KILLING WITH PREJUDICE

Killing with Prejudice

*Institutionalized Racism in
American Capital Punishment*

R. J. Maratea

NEW YORK UNIVERSITY PRESS
New York

NEW YORK UNIVERSITY PRESS
New York
www.nyupress.org

Library of Congress Cataloging-in-Publication Data
Names: Maratea, R. J., 1973–, author.
Title: Killing with prejudice : institutionalized racism in American capital
punishment / R. J. Maratea.
Description: New York : New York University Press, 2019. |
Includes bibliographical references and index.
Identifiers: LCCN 2018020941 | ISBN 9781479888603 (cl : alk. paper)
Subjects: LCSH: Capital punishment—United States. | Discrimination in
capital punishment—United States. | Discrimination in criminal justice
administration—United States. | Racism—United States.
Classification: LCC KF9227.C2 M37 2018 | DDC 364.66089/96073—dc23
LC record available at https://lccn.loc.gov/2018020941

New York University Press books are printed on acid-free paper, and their
binding materials are chosen for strength and durability. We strive to use
environmentally responsible suppliers and materials to the greatest extent
possible in publishing our books.

Manufactured in the United States of America

10 9 8 7 6 5 4 3 2 1

Also available as an ebook

To Freddy and Sofie

CONTENTS

FIGURES AND TABLES

FIGURES

TABLES

Introduction

Bifurcated Justice in the Deep South

On September 25, 1991, Warren McCleskey was executed in the death chamber at the Georgia Diagnostic and Classification Prison. The culmination of a 13-year litigation process that twice reached the United States Supreme Court, McCleskey's closing moments were as chaotic and discomforting as many of the legal decisions that preceded his death. After a series of last-minute appeals were denied and his legal options exhausted, McCleskey—who at one point had been secured to the death chair only to be removed minutes later while his lawyers tried desperately to delay the execution—refused his last meal and made a final statement: "I pray that one day this country, supposedly a civilized society, will abolish barbaric acts such as the death penalty" (Applebome 1991:A18). With the Georgia Department of Pardons and Parole having denied a clemency petition and the Supreme Court rejecting one final request for a stay, Warren McCleskey was "strapped into the electric chair, electrodes attached to his skull and a final prayer read. . . . A minute later the execution began, and he was pronounced dead at 3:13 [a.m.]" (Applebome 1991).

This book chronicles the journey of Warren McCleskey from an innocuous criminal to the symbolic figure whose legal plight and execution underscores the lingering racial and socioeconomic inequalities endemic to capital punishment in the United States. The modern death penalty as it exists in the United States has been inexorably shaped by the state of Georgia and the Supreme Court decision in *McCleskey v. Kemp* (1987)—the legal ruling at the heart of this story—which affirmed institutionalized racial disparities as acceptable components in a functioning capital punishment system. Despite the gravity of Warren McCleskey's case, he has become an obscure figure in the decades since his death. Yet *McCleskey v. Kemp* sheds important light on the unwillingness of the judiciary to meaningfully address inequity in the justice system. Although the proverbial *color line* is deeply embedded in Georgia's legal institution—serving as a powerful predictor of wrongful conviction and disproportionate sentencing—the Supreme Court in *McCleskey* chose to overlook compelling empirical evidence revealing the discriminatory manner in which the assailants of black Americans are systematically undercharged and the aggressors of white victims are far more likely to receive a death sentence.

Warren McCleskey might seem like an unlikely candidate to expose the frailties and failures of U.S. capital punishment. He was hardly someone who could be cast as a sympathetic figure, having had a string of arrests prior to that fateful day on May 13, 1978, when he and three accomplices—Ben Wright, David Burney, and Bernard Depree—arrived at the Dixie Furniture Store in Atlanta, Georgia, with the intention of committing armed robbery. As McCleskey entered through the front door and secured the area by forcing anyone present to lie face down on the floor, the others came through a loading dock in the rear of the store, where they searched the premises for cash. Although the robbers tied up all of the employees and customers—even threatening to kill anyone who moved—one had already managed to trigger the silent alarm; police were quickly dispatched to the scene. Officer Frank Schlatt, a five-year veteran on the Atlanta police force, was the first to respond, parking his patrol car near the store and entering through the front door. According to court records, McCleskey noticed Schlatt arrive and quickly hid behind a couch on the showroom floor. As Schlatt maneuvered his way down an aisle in the middle of the store, McCleskey allegedly leaped up and fired two shots in Schlatt's direction. The first struck the 30-year-old officer in the head, causing his death; the second ricocheted off a cigarette lighter in the left chest pocket of Schlatt's uniform. As McCleskey and his accomplices fled the scene, Officer Schlatt fell to the floor into a pool of his own blood; he was pronounced dead several hours later. McCleskey was eventually arrested for Schlatt's murder a few weeks later, after being apprehended for an unrelated crime (*McCleskey v. Zant*, 580 F. Supp. 338, 345 (1984)).

It did not take long for the authorities to pinpoint McCleskey as the perpetrator in Officer Schlatt's murder. Two employees of the Dixie Furniture Store identified McCleskey as the robber who had entered through the front door. Although McCleskey's defense attorney, John Turner Jr., offered an unsubstantiated alibi defense during trial (*Zant*, 580 F. Supp. at 346), McCleskey in his confession statement to police never disputed the fact that he had participated in the crime but adamantly denied being the gunman who had shot and killed Officer Schlatt (see Kirchmeier 2015).[1] Nevertheless, jurors were confronted with damning evidence of McCleskey's guilt: "One of his accomplices, Ben Wright, testified that McCleskey admitted to shooting the officer. A jail inmate housed near McCleskey testified that McCleskey made a 'jail house confession' in which he claimed he was the triggerman. The police officer was killed by a bullet fired from a .38 caliber Rossi handgun. McCleskey had stolen a .38 caliber Rossi in a previous holdup" (*McCleskey v. Kemp*, 753

F.2d 877, 882 (1985)). The jury of 11 whites and one African American ultimately found McCleskey guilty of first-degree murder and two counts of armed robbery.[2] We may presume that the murder conviction was at least partly influenced by the testimony of accomplice Ben Wright and the jailhouse informant, Offie Gene Evans, both of whom told jurors that McCleskey was the lone gunman, and Wright's claim that McCleskey had in his possession a .38 caliber silver pistol that matched the bullet used to kill Officer Schlatt (Kirchmeier 2015). Yet not all of the evidence presented during trial was conclusive. Two of the Dixie employees had seen McCleskey enter the store, but neither could identify him as the shooter; and while the gun used to kill Officer Schlatt was linked to McCleskey, it was never found by police and could have been fired by any one of the four offenders present at the time of the crime. In fact, during cross-examination by Turner, Ben Wright admitted to having a .38 caliber revolver, and "when police arrested Wright's girlfriend, she claimed Wright carried a .38 and McCleskey carried a .45 weapon" (Kirchmeier 2015:22).

None of this is meant to suggest that McCleskey was wrongly convicted, as there was compelling evidence that he did, in fact, fire the bullet that killed Officer Schlatt. Some readers may even wonder why anyone should focus on such a seemingly unsympathetic figure at the risk of trivializing the death and memory of Frank Schlatt, a respected Atlanta police officer, husband, and father whose friends and family are undoubtedly as pained today by his loss as they were in the immediate aftermath of his murder. In truth, this book could be about any one of a number of death-row inmates whom most people have never heard of and whose stories of innocence or guilt do not even register in the public consciousness. But the costs and consequences of the death penalty exist beyond the relative value (or lack thereof) of any single person. Instead, we must place capital punishment in historical context in order to better understand how Warren McCleskey's particular experience is neither unique nor constitutionally acceptable regardless of whether he was actually guilty of the crime for which he was executed.

Slave Codes, Black Codes, Jim Crow, and Then McCleskey

The murder of a white police officer was a grievous offense that hit squarely in the face of expected racial etiquette in the Deep South and singled out Warren McCleskey as a black man in need of killing. The crime itself also reflected the historical bifurcation of justice administration—one for whites and another for nonwhites—inherent to the sentencing system in Georgia, as argued by McCleskey's appellate counsel, Jack Boger:

> If the State of Georgia had criminal statutes that expressly imposed different penalties, harsher penalties, on black defendants simply because they were black, or on those who killed white victims, simply because those victims were white, the statutes would plainly violate the Constitution. There was a time, of course, when the State of Georgia did have such statutes, before our nation's Civil War, when free blacks and slaves alike could be given a death sentence merely for the crime of assault on a Georgia white citizen. With the ratification of the Fourteenth Amendment, such criminal statutes came explicitly no longer to be written. Yet the old habits of mind, the racial attitudes of that time have survived, as this Court well knows, into the current century. Today, we are before the Court with a substantial body of evidence indicat-

ing that during the last decade Georgia prosecutors and juries, in their administration of Georgia's post-Furman capital statutes, have continued to act as if some of those old statutes were still on the books. (*McCleskey v. Kemp*, No. 84-6811 (oral arguments Oct. 15, 1986), at 0:17)

Boger's point is that Georgia's contemporary implementation of capital punishment reflects a continuation of historical attitudes that preceded the Civil War and persist, albeit often unconsciously, "in the minds of prosecutors and jurors" (Poveda 2016:24). The racial beliefs in question reflect a social arrangement tasked simultaneously to protect the lives of whites and to discipline African Americans in the traditional fashion as slave and black codes had operated in the antebellum and Reconstruction periods, respectively.[3] Since the slave-owning colonies were largely arranged along the Atlantic and Gulf of Mexico coastlines, they were adjacent to ready supplies of marketable slaves from the Caribbean Basin and South America, from which millions of slaves were absorbed into the U.S. South.

The ideology and practice of human servitude was a notion prominent in Western civilization since ancient Greece, where its ideal type was socially and politically dead chattel, forcibly removed from kith and kin, bought and sold as one would livestock, with no rights, manners, or thoughts that free citizens were wont to respect. Slaves in Greece and Rome were numerous and vital as agricultural labor engines (*familia rustica*) but also functioned as educators, managers, physicians, publicans (*servus publicus*), and *helots*. In Rome, slaves were often debt bondpeople who worked off their debts and bought their freedom. Epictetus the Stoic was a slave. Aesop was a slave. Seneca advocated for the humane treatment of slaves,[4] which probably influenced Emperor

Nero's directive that courts receive complaints against unjust masters (Cobb 1858; Stephens 1997);[5] and Antoninus Pius mandated owners who killed their slaves "without cause" to be tried as murderers (Hunt 2018:204). Although there was great variance in the potential life chances of the enslaved, it is widely recognized that slavery was an institution of economic necessity in the Roman Empire.

U.S. slaveholders were keenly aware of slavery's importance to their own economic well-being, but that fact was the only commonality that the U.S. institution retained as a remnant of the classical world. White southerners perhaps wished to think of slavery in their instance as distinct from that of Greece or Rome, but it was no less harsh and deeply dehumanizing. As the numbers of bondpeople grew with imports from Africa before 1808 and the slave stock realized a natural increase, the U.S. South recognized a need for legal structures governing the control and punishment of slaves, a status increasingly identified with blackness by 1680 and exclusively tied to race by 1700. The governing acts known as slave codes were essentially *black* slave codes. The Commonwealth of Virginia, being England's first colony established in North America and the first to import slaves, was a template for many slave codes written later. Although the codification of legal guidelines for slavery seemed to legitimate its existence, more than a few Virginians, even slave owners such as Thomas Jefferson, harbored personal distain of slavery, wished to abolish it, and blamed South Carolinians, Georgians, and some well-placed New Englanders for the stubborn resistance on behalf of slavery when the American Revolution began (Waldstreicher 2009). With the victory of Washington over Lord Cornwallis at Yorktown in 1781, slaves were often considered spoils of war. The British had promised freedom to any slave who took arms against rebels (i.e., their masters), so when the war ended, slaves were considered emblematic of tyranny and far from any sentiment leading to freedom.

In the ensuing decades, Georgians were securely in favor of slavery and backed the sectionalist parties that it spawned, in part because of their geography, which was located away from any border with a potentially hostile northern state. Jefferson in the final decades of his life implored Virginians to abolish slavery because if a sectional war over it occurred, Virginia would be a battleground in such a conflict. He was correct. His warnings should have been overheard in Georgia. Nevertheless, Georgians were pleased with the Constitution, which protected slavery, and voted to accept it unanimously (Waldstreicher 2009). The geographic center of the black population in bondage was in Georgia and further concentrated in the Deep South, which not coincidentally was also the epicenter of lynching in the decades to come (Klein 1971). The pattern of sentiments pertaining to slavery in Georgia and throughout the Deep South was one of deepening severity punctuated by periods of crisis when rules were liberalized. During the Revolutionary War, when there was an attempt to reconcile slaves to the emerging confederation of states, and in the Civil War, when a movement for humanitarian reform emerged within the Confederacy (Genovese 1972), there were periods of reprieve from the humiliation and cruelty that characterized the day-to-day life for those who were in bondage.

Aside from the haphazard living conditions, precarious family attachments, and rather perilous personal circumstances of black bondpeople, they had considerable value as regenerative commodities in which investments might appreciate in a microeconomic sense. They provided a macroeconomic benefit as well. The great compromise realized by the installation of the three-fifths clause ensured that taxation would be eased with the addition of slaves to the census and also promised faster and wider expansion into the western territories (e.g., Alabama, Tennessee, Kentucky, and Mississippi). The lands acquired in 1804 beyond the Mississippi River in the Louisiana Purchase and on into the Mexican Cession after 1848 presented a potential for slavery's expansion that both awed and alarmed abolitionists, most of all in its promise to create a political imbalance in the Congress built around a market in human beings.

Slave Laws of 1682

Considering the large numbers of slaves relative to whites—by 1700 slaves were almost entirely blacks from Africa, the Caribbean, or South America—it seems logical that owners and planters, as well as transporters, wholesalers, and marketers of slaves, would be anxious to regulate their behaviors and relationships with white free populations, as well as settle the uncertainties of people-property in southern society. Although the first Africans brought to North America were considered indentured servants (in that they had a term of service that elapsed), by 1640 those who were imported were considered bondpeople for life and their children the same. Several conventions regarding the keeping of servants and the maintenance of institutional slavery emerged over the period between 1640 and 1682:

- 1662: Children born to black slave women were bonded to their owner.
- 1667: Baptizing slaves as Christians did not alter a slave's status or that of her children.
- 1669: An owner who killed a disobedient slave would not be tried for committing a felony.

- 1670: Free blacks and Native Americans were prohibited from buying slaves or indentured servants. This rule lapsed, and many Native Americans who owned land were encouraged by European colonists to purchase slaves and participate in the slave trade (Onion 2016).[6]
- 1680: Slaves were prohibited from carrying weapons and could not leave their owner's plantation without a written pass.
- 1682: No master or overseer could permit another person's slave to remain on his or her plantation for longer than four hours without the permission of the slave's owner.
- 1691: If a white man or woman married a black person, mulatto, or Indian, he or she was banished from Virginia and later from Georgia, Florida, and Alabama.[7]

In large part, the rules accompanying slavery grew more rigid and covered every aspect of a slave's life: "Given this background, the legislation of the nineteenth century would prove in many ways even more detrimental to slave rights than all the preceding enactments of the slave code. For these codes assumed that the Negro was an inferior being, and to maintain him in his docility and obedience, denied him every possible access to independence and avenue for self expression" (Klein 1967:54–55).

Slavery, if not bogged down by sentiment or encumbered by affection or sympathy, could be lucrative, as a slave, both as a unit of labor and as a reproductive entity, held great value (see Genovese 1972). It was necessary to view slaves as entities of production and shares of investment. Living conditions suffered in such an environment. Although the slave codes allowed considerable latitude in regard to conditions under which slave owners might utilize their property—Georgia's not being exceptional among them—legal bifurcation usually worked to the disadvantage of bondpeople, in that drivers and masters were negligent, pitiless, or, in more instances than decent people wish to acknowledge, sadistic. However, the codes also allowed slave owners to dictate circumstances under which their property could be used in their absence or held after their deaths. Although uncommon, owners occasionally left explicit instructions for the care and conditions under which a favorite slave could serve, where and with whom particular slaves might be quartered, and what sort of work they might be tasked to complete (Stampp 1956). More often, codification of traditional slavery practices in Georgia as well as in other states spoke to the intrinsic and potential economic value of slaves and the necessity of preserving their life and limb when at all possible.

When slavery and the market for slaves were abolished following the Civil War, both the potential value and the need to protect slaves vanished. Freedpeople were surplus labor existing in an imposed state of ignorance, in large part as a result of slave codes that prohibited even the most rudimentary education, forbade any travel or even passive knowledge of the world, and deprived them of any historical or family legacies outside of superstitions and folklore. It is difficult to bring to mind any one group of people so abruptly thrust on the world in such unprepared, unprotected, and thoughtless circumstances. Freedpeople experienced a reception characterized by violence and terrorism that is comparable to some of the worst examples of human cruelty on record. The treatment of black Americans from the end of Reconstruction through the waning of the civil rights movement is an exemplar for social regression. When Europeans were realizing a rationalization of punishments, transitioning away from spectacles of cruelty that functioned as both social control and a form of entertainment to the *gentler* way of punishing through the use of incarceration, rehabilitation, and social hygiene (see Foucault [1977] 1995), black Americans experienced a regime of race-based terrorism so deeply rooted that it marked families indelibly and constructed a gulf of separation so deep that it remains a sore subject today.

The colony of Georgia was ambivalent about the presence of slaves and suspicious of slave trading to a degree that during the 1700s, colonial authorities banned the institution, eventually settling on a slave economy that also became the destination for English, Irish, and Scots exiled from the British Isles. In turn, Florida adopted most of Georgia's code; Alabama similarly embraced it in 1833. All of those included the following provisions:

- Slaves were forbidden to leave the owner's property unless accompanied by a white person or with written permission. In the event a slave left his or her owner's property without permission, every white person was required to chastise them, capture them, or at least report their whereabouts to the civilian posse.
- Any slave attempting to run away and leave the colony (later, the state) received the death penalty, although it was rarely exacted on the offender.
- Any slave who evaded capture for 20 days or more was to be publicly whipped for the first offense, branded with an "R" on the right cheek on the second offense, lose one ear if absent for 30 days on the third offense, and castrated on the fourth offense.
- Owners refusing to abide by the slave code were fined and forfeited their slaves.

- Slave homes were subject to be searched intermittently for weapons, reading/writing materials, or plans for insurrection. Punishment ranged from loss of an ear, branding, and nose slitting to hanging after a repeat offense.
- Although frequently rented out to reliable businesspeople, slaves could not be clerks or work in any capacity that required finer clothing. The fear was that they would be taken for freedpeople.
- Alcoholic beverages were prohibited to slaves.

There were laws punishing whites for harming their slaves, but these were rare and haphazardly enforced or easily avoided. One of the truest forms of legal bifurcation was rape laws in the South. They embodied a race-based double standard that permitted slave women to be victimized at will, while male slaves were sanctioned on the single word of a white accuser; and whereas white men could rape female slaves with relative impunity, black men accused of rape were put to death during the antebellum period.

Black Codes and Bifurcated Justice

It stands to reason that the openly racist bifurcations in antebellum law were manifested and supported by governmental and legal institutions. Still, the Reconstruction decades following the Civil War witnessed changes in Georgia law that effectively created second-class citizenship for black Americans and permitted the erection of a segregated society with a multitiered criminal justice system. After the Civil War, white southerners moved quickly to eliminate black people's newfound freedom. In order to do this legally, the legislatures of the former Confederate states passed new laws that appeared, on the surface, to be neutral and fair to all races but were actually designed to repress black people. At the outset of Reconstruction, these laws were called Black Codes because of their similarity to the slave codes that they sought to replace. It is important to remember and continuously recall that racial segregation was not a new thing in Georgia. Antebellum slavery fixed the status and circumstance of most black Americans (whether free or in bondage), leaving little need for statutory measures segregating the races. This pre-Reconstruction slave caste did not survive and was replaced by post–Civil War Black Codes that outraged some people in the North because it seemed that the southern states were creating a form of quasi-slavery to negate the results of the war. After winning large majorities in the 1866 elections, the Republicans put the South under military rule. They held new elections in which freedmen could vote, suffrage was expanded to poor whites, and all the postwar Black Codes were repealed. Moreover, the 14th Amendment's Equal Protection Clause and extension of due process to state jurisdictions ensured that Black Codes could not reappear in southern lawmaking (Litwack 1998).

By 1877, however, new legislation effectively narrowed the civil rights and liberties of black Americans to circumstances very similar to the conditions of bondage that existed before emancipation. When Union forces that had been occupying Georgia for 12 years left the South following the inauguration of Rutherford B. Hayes as president in March 1877, white Georgians reenacted every aspect of the former Black Codes. The legislation was intended to continue the traditional disparate treatment of black persons, who were excluded from public education, could not vote or serve on juries, and were cut off from professions that potentially might serve whites, including medicine, law, and civil service positions. Even though discriminatory laws against blacks existed in both northern and southern states from the early 19th century, the term "Black Codes" specifically referred to laws passed by southern state legislatures at the end of the Civil War to control the labor, social behavior, civic participation, and movement of freedpeople. Reflecting the unwillingness of white southerners to accept blacks as equals, the codes reaffirmed the inferior position of freedpeople by establishing a legal system that underscored the color line separating whites and blacks.

These discrepancies were further emphasized following the Supreme Court's decision to uphold the constitutionality of state laws mandating racial segregation under the doctrine of *separate but equal* in *Plessy v. Ferguson* (1896), which inspired the ratification of Jim Crow throughout the South. In Georgia, Jim Crow laws were seen as effective tools for controlling freedpeople; and while they were oppressive, they did not address—and by default guaranteed—certain rights, such as legalized marriage, ownership of property, and some access to the courts. However, black Americans could not testify against whites, serve on juries or in state militias, carry knives or firearms unless they were licensed, and vote. Some laws also declared that those who failed to sign yearly labor contracts could be arrested and hired out to white landowners. Several states limited the occupations open to black Americans and barred them from acquiring land, and others provided that judges could impose heavy sentences on black men. Furthermore, black vagrants were fined heavily and, if they could not pay the sum, were hired out to service until the claim was satisfied. The laws were tested initially in *Breedlove v. Suttles* (1937), in which the High Court ruled that a Georgia poll tax permitting the state to disenfranchise black voters was constitutional. W. E. B. DuBois ([1935] 1992) commented that these Jim Crow–era Black Codes had been enacted to "keep the Negroes in their positions and reduce the numbers of beggars and thieves" (167).

The supposed deficits of black citizens in intellectual, moral, and civil sensitivities were such that many Georgians felt that one uniform code for all persons, white and black, could never be realized (see Talmadge 1955). That opinion prevailed among a vast majority of white Georgians for a century, institutionalizing segregation and permitting unequal subsystems of education, health care, religion, and, importantly, criminal justice that promoted the interests of whites over blacks. Similarly, civil authorities turned a blind eye to white vigilantism intended to discipline, terrorize, and demoralize black Americans. These circumstances thrived until the late 1960s, when federal intervention enforced a number of civil rights mandates striking down state laws and municipal ordinances outlawing miscegenation and segregating schools, public facilities, and transportation. Nonetheless, the Supreme Court's decision to allow Georgia to resume executions following *Gregg v. Georgia* (1976) and later to deny relief in *McCleskey v. Kemp* (1987) ignored clear statistical evidence that the civil and legal bifurcations of segregated, Jim Crow Georgia were still a reality.

This was precisely the argument put forth by Warren McCleskey's lead counsel, Jack Boger, in stating that Georgia's capital system functions "as if some of those old statutes were still on the books" (*McCleskey*, No. 84-6811, at 1:07). The troublesome nature of the Court's legal reasoning in *McCleskey*, which is chronicled throughout the book, underscores the undeniable reality that capital punishment has borne a close resemblance to lynching in Georgia, where more extralegal executions of black Americans occurred than in any other state. "The merger between the two is the phenom-enon known as legal lynching," according to the historian William S. McFeely (1997), who points out that "as killings outside the law declined in the twentieth century South, the infliction of the death penalty by the courts increased." The well-documented existence of pervasive racial disparities in various phases of the capital punishment process is part and parcel of the Court's logic in the *McCleskey* ruling and locates that case in the great and ongoing struggle for ideological ascendancy on issue of race in the United States. As we shall see, the Supreme Court disregarded the detailed and peer-reviewed statistical evidence of disparate treatment of black Americans in Georgia presented by McCleskey's lawyers, choosing instead to send the message that overt forms of dis-parity were no longer permitted but less tangible techniques of institutional racism would be tolerated. Notwithstanding that the state of Georgia was caught red-handed applying its laws in a fashion that had always been regarded as discrimi-natory, the Court effectively "immunized the criminal justice system from judicial scrutiny for racial bias" (Michelle Alex-ander, on *Bill Moyers Journal* 2010).

Decades later, the *McCleskey* decision continues to un-derscore the lingering racial, socioeconomic, and gendered inequalities endemic to U.S. capital punishment and pro-foundly reflects the character of our justice system more generally. The case is so important that the distinguished legal scholar Anthony Amsterdam described the ruling as "the Dred Scott decision of our time" (Liptak 2008); and the *New York Times* labeled it as one of the more troubling Su-preme Court rulings of the late 20th century: "Confronted with powerful evidence that racial feelings play a large part in determining who will live and who will die, the Court . . . effectively condoned the expression of racism in a profound aspect of our law" (Lewis 1987:A31). This duality in justice administration situates Warren McCleskey's behavior as the black assailant of a white man in relation to both the dominant racial discourse and legal environment that are fundamentally relevant in understanding how the ultimate punishment functions for defendants, for victims, and within the U.S. justice system as a whole.

1

Reconstruction, Jim Crow, and the New Segregation

Gunnar Myrdal, in his famous *An American Dilemma* (1944), saw democracy triumphing over racist discrimination. He argued that incremental advancements in the lives and status of black Americans would initiate a cycle of improvement in the general welfare of blacks that would eventually disprove stereotypical notions of blacks' inferiority. In some ways, history has proven Myrdal's vision accurate with regard to integration and institutional reforms, which have expanded opportunity and functioned to enhance the quality of life for many people of color. Yet his *principle of cumulation* overlooks the fact that "targeting only one aspect of a system of structural racism would fail to help the black underclass . . . unless there was a concerted effort to address simultaneously all of the interlocking problems of political powerless, jobs, education, and crime" (Jackson 1990:197). Warren McCleskey's life, which began during an era of legal apartheid and spanned through the civil rights movement and beyond the presidency of Jimmy Carter, a white Georgian who advocates for racial equality and civil rights, exemplified this paradox of social progress for black Americans.

At the time of McCleskey's birth on March 17, 1946, the last vestiges of Jim Crow were still firmly in place. The Ku Klux Klan was actively promoting the virtues of white supremacy, and segregation epitomized the prevailing culture of black contemptibility that characterized life in Georgia and throughout the nation. By this time, whites had perfected a racial order that protected "their economic, political, and social interests in a world without slavery" or convict-lease (M. Alexander 2010:32), and they were intent on preserving the racial equilibrium attained via segregation without any federal interference through constitutional remakes, judicial decisions, and statutory remedies. Through the passage of Black Codes and other segregation laws, white elites sought to disintegrate the possibility of political alliances among disenfranchised blacks and lower-class whites: "As long as poor whites directed their hatred and frustration against the black competitor, the planters were relieved of class hostility directed against them" (W. Wilson 1978:54; see also M. Alexander 2010).

With political leaders such as Georgia's Governor Herman Talmadge preaching to marginalized and underprivileged whites that the "tradition of segregation in the South . . . has proven itself to the best interest of both races" (1955:5), blacks were powerless to oppose the system of racial caste thrust on them through Jim Crow.[1] Michelle Alexander notes that during the early 20th century, every southern state "had laws on the books that disenfranchised blacks and discriminated against them in virtually every sphere of public life, lending sanction to a racial ostracism that extended to schools, churches, housing, jobs" and an array of other public spaces (2010:35), helping to ensure that blacks were red-lined into crime-ridden slums. Warren McCleskey's youth was indeed characterized by poverty and surrounded by violence. Raised in an impoverished neighborhood of Marietta, Georgia, McCleskey never knew his birth father but was exposed from a young age to a violent upbringing, both in his community and in his household (Curriden 1991). He lived for a time with his aunt, who often beat him physically; and his stepfather, John Henry Brooks, would often violently abuse McCleskey, his siblings, and their mother, Willie Mae, during drunken rages. His mother and stepfather also exposed him to various forms of vice from a young age; this included selling bootlegged moonshine and operating an illegal gambling den from their home (see Kirchmeier 2015).

> The violence was terrifying and never-ending. About every weekend, someone in the neighborhood was shot and killed. Fights all the time. A dog-eat-dog world where only the strong survive. . . . My childhood was very rough. Very, very poor. . . . The hardest was the violence we grew up in as a family. It was a skid-row type neighborhood in Marietta. We sold white lightning out of our house. In 1963, my stepfather threatened to kill my mother. Out of fear, she grabbed a pistol under a mattress in the living room and shot it several times. I walked in the door seconds later, and he was dead. (*Atlanta Journal and Constitution* 1991:A12; see also Curriden 1991:A1)[2]

With McCleskey being surrounded by violence and with little hope of escaping the poverty of the Marietta slums, it is perhaps unsurprising that he turned to crime in order to achieve a degree of financial stability. After all, at this time the Ku Klux Klan and other prominent whites openly opposed desegregation and any opportunities for blacks to integrate into middle-class, white southern society.

Despite all of these setbacks and roadblocks, McCleskey graduated from his segregated high school in 1964 and shortly after married his girlfriend, Gwendolyn Carmichael, who gave birth to their daughter, Carla, two years later in 1966. In order for McCleskey to support his young family, he was employed for a time at a Lockheed aircraft plant outside

Atlanta, only to be laid off in 1969 (Curriden 1991). Unable to subsequently find steady employment, McCleskey was so destitute by 1970 that his wife threatened to take his daughter and leave him, the fear of which compelled him to commit a string of nine armed robberies (Curriden 1991; Kirchmeier 2015). Within a matter of weeks, McCleskey was arrested, pleaded guilty, and was sentenced to three life terms for his crimes. His sentence was ultimately reduced on appeal, however, and he was eventually paroled after seven years. "'When I got out in 1977, I had a vision. I wanted to get back on my feet and reunited with my family,' [McCleskey] said. 'I thought if I could get ahold of a little money, I could get that to come to pass'" (Curriden 1991:A1).

Upon his release, McCleskey had hoped to reconcile with his family and achieve financial security outside prison. But securing employment with a felony record proved a difficult task for McCleskey. Within a year, he and his wife had divorced, and "his life started spiraling out of control" (Kirchmeier 2015:13). During this time, he began abusing drugs and became friends with David Burney, Bernard Depree, and Ben Wright, who each had their own considerable criminal records (see Kirchmeier 2015). It was alongside these accomplices that McCleskey participated in a string of robberies in and around Atlanta, including the ill-fated May 13, 1978, Dixie Furniture Store robbery during which the responding officer Frank Schlatt was fatally shot. McCleskey's subsequent arrest on two counts of armed robbery and one count of murder set in motion one of the most consequential legal battles of the late 20th century and has come to embody the shifting nature of racial discrimination from the perspicuous bias of the Jim Crow era to the more subtle forms of prejudice that pervade contemporary U.S. society.

The Politics of Jim Crow Justice

By 1943, Georgia's Governor Ellis Arnall had already set in motion a series of civil rights reforms, which included the abolishment of the state poll tax and revocation of the Ku Klux Klan's corporate charter (Wexler 2003). As if this were not enough to rouse the fear of southerners keen on protecting Georgia's segregationist tradition, by the middle of the decade, many northerners had concluded that Jim Crow laws were unsustainable and would have to be reformed or abolished in their entirety. Unwilling to accept the idea of reformation, segregationists were only convinced by these events to begrudgingly retrench and adopt modifications that would allow traditional racist principles to flourish without overtly visible discrimination from social, cultural, and political institutions (see Keys and Maratea 2016).[3] Michelle Alexander notes that "the seeds for the new system of control were planted well before the end of the Civil Rights Movement. A new race-neutral language was developed for appealing to old racist sentiments, a language accompanied by a political movement that succeeded in putting the vast majority of blacks back in their place. Proponents of racial hierarchy found they could install a new racial caste system without violating the law or the new limits of acceptable political discourse, by demanding 'law and order' rather than 'segregation forever'" (2010:40). In the decades following the civil rights movement, explicit reference to racial divisions was supplanted by official color blindness, race neutrality, and nominal equality. However, a predominant culture of crypto-segregation continues to thrive in convention and custom.

Before 1968, miscegenation laws, restrictive covenants governing residential property, and employment and educational segregation worked in concert with a nearly unshakable ethos of separation and illusory black inferiority, which many white southerners then and now understand as a historical legacy and conventional wage of whiteness. In Georgia, the 159 separate counties spread over 57,906 square miles have traditionally had broad powers, with a relatively free hand in regulating educational, political, legal, and cultural matters. This political arrangement proved particularly effective at allowing Black Codes and other unwritten policies of racial disenfranchisement to be carried out as cooperative agreements among and between county personnel, a system in which responsibility for enforcement was dispersed among an array of local entities, each of whom had limited accountability. County sheriffs, for example, routinely overlooked or participated in the lynching of blacks and then were tasked with facilitating investigations that inevitably concluded that the victims had died at the hands of parties unknown (see *Chicago Defender* 1937a). Likewise, restrictions on voting rights and exclusion from officeholding could easily be enforced by installing a determined and "ideologically functional" clerk in the county courthouse. As long as each jurisdiction had support from the state house and realized no interference from indifferent or distantly placed federal authorities, discriminatory practices such as segregation could remain in place.

If affected black American or "nigger-loving" whites protested, local supporters of segregation, hastily assembled vigilante mobs, or even the Ku Klux Klan—whose members sometimes operated local law enforcement—would regularly apply force adequate to the task of silencing them. Georgia in particular witnessed regular incidents of lynching—with 531 chronicled events between 1882 and 1968—along with thousands of less-than-deadly assaults, disappearances, threats, and acts of intimidation delivered anonymously or by police (Tuskegee University Archives Repository 2010).

> For the men and women who composed these mobs, as for those who remained silent and indifferent or who provided scholarly or scientific explanations, this was the highest idealism in the service of their race. One has only to view the self-satisfied expression on their faces as they posed beneath black people hanging from a rope or next to the charred remains of a Negro who had been burned to death. What is more disturbing about these scenes is the discovery that the perpetrators of the crimes were ordinary people, not so different from ourselves—merchants, farmers, laborers, machine operators, teachers, doctors, lawyers, policemen, students; they were family men and women, good churchgoing folk who came to believe that keeping black people in their place was nothing less than pest control, a way of combating an epidemic or virus that if not checked would be detrimental to the health and security of the community. (Litwack 1998:122)

The state of Georgia actively assisted local jurisdictions in limiting civil rights by aggressively fighting efforts to enact federal antilynching legislation, instituting cumulative poll taxes (1877), using white primary elections (1900), and establishing literacy tests (1908). By invoking the necessity to preserve states' rights, southerners unwilling "to sacrifice the virtue of Southern womanhood and mongrelize the race" were fighting against northerners trying to "infuriate the South" by appeasing "radical Negroes who want social rights with whites" (*Chicago Defender* 1940a:2). In practice, the argument was little more than a euphemism for exempting state government from the ramifications of an individual county's application of law and reaffirming the state's entitlement to treat its citizens as it wished.

Georgia officials perhaps assumed that the federal government was unable or unwilling to interfere in the operations of state or local affairs following the U.S. Supreme Court's decision in *United States v. Cruikshank* (1875), in which indictments were dismissed against individuals who had murdered more than 100 black Americans assembled in support of Republican candidates during the 1872 Louisiana gubernatorial election. Citing federal authorities for failure to identify a constitutional right that had been violated, the majority justices ignored the First Amendment's guarantee of free assembly and overlooked the unconstitutional motivation of deliberate racial discrimination in the electoral process, stating that such an indictment was valid only when applied to the states, not individuals. In effect, the decision in *Cruikshank* "rendered national prosecution of crimes against blacks virtually impossible, and gave a green light to acts of terror where local officials either could not or would not enforce the law" (Foner 1988:531).

Lynching flourished, emerging as more than a mechanism for dispensing justice in the South; it also reflected the rampant institutionalization of injustice and inequality in U.S. society. Whereas public officials such as Georgia governor Allen D. Chandler openly endorsed lynching "as a method of controlling black criminality" (Dray 2002:4) and community leaders often participated in the lynching of blacks—or were too fearful to intervene and stop the killings—federal politicians and northern legislators tacitly condoned the practice by failing to take any meaningful action.

There has been much debate over the attempted passage of numerous anti-lynching bills. Many have been the vindications made in defense of legislators responsible for this inglorious defeat; but no justifiable reasons given for their failure of passage. . . . Somehow, not one of these bills has become law. Prejudiced representatives from the South, coupled with general disinterest on the part of many northern representatives who do not come from districts where Race voters are such an integral part, plus the general vote-trading on various legislation favorable to certain committees are the governing factors in the defeat of these bills. (Abbott 1936:1)

Since the prominent white majority in the South favored lynching and the elimination of mob justice was not a foremost political priority for many liberal whites, the terrorism of blacks continued unabated throughout the South during the first four decades of the 20th century. The bigotry was so widespread that only 1 percent of known lynchings ever resulted in a criminal conviction (*Chicago Defender* 1938a): Jurors often secured bogus verdicts; authorities tended to lie about or "forget" the details of a lynch party when testifying; and the systemic institutionalization of inequality throughout the South, and in the U.S. more generally, ensured that courtroom trials would be no less discriminatory than a lynching.

By the late 1930s, however, the sheer barbarism of brazen public lynch mobs had become a rallying point for the abolition movement. Growing public discontent and the prominence of antilynching campaigns, both within and outside the U.S. South, gradually eased the heretofore-ubiquitous threat of extralegal racial violence against black Americans. As lynching declined, southern states turned to their criminal justice operatives. Status quo courts and juries that harbored no affection for disenfranchised blacks legitimized criminal prosecutions and sentencing, which traditionally turned on (white) authorities' initiative and enforcement preferences (Keys and Maratea 2016). They were convenient mechanisms for advancing segregationist ideology. Georgia proved to be a regrettable example of blacks' inability to forge functional political alliances with white Republicans, precipitating a hostile political environment that frowned on race mixing in social institutions.

Georgia's enduring determination to relegate black Americans to a status ensuring a passive dependence on white prerogatives is documented throughout the decades from Reconstruction through the 1970s. Pre-*Furman* executions demonstrate one of the clearest images of racial subjugation, but the state legislature's continuing support for discriminatory policies in education, public transportation, and accommodations, as well as antimiscegenation laws, reveal a particular desire as late as 1961 to disproportionately oppress black Georgians (see Ga. Code Ann. § 53-106 (1961), outlawing interracial marriage). The threat of miscegenation and the peril of interracial violence and homicide—specifically crimes committed by a black assailant against a white victim—were closely tied together in the decades following the Civil War and similarly punished by death. Outside of formulating statutes and perpetuating customs pertaining to sexual relations and hostile conflict, the state of Georgia was endeavoring to separate the races as best as it could and in doing so establish bifurcated institutions wherever possible.

Practical and Symbolic Executions

As a century passed following the Civil War and the civil rights movement acquired a wider legitimacy of its own, local law enforcement and segregated juries remained the single bastions of racial discipline exempt from progressive changes in the state's legal code forbidding discrimination in employment, housing, public accommodations, transportation, and education. Overt acts of intolerance declined, replaced by more sterile and discreet forms of generalized institutional racism. When the Civil Rights Act of 1964 and the Voting Rights Act of 1965 became the law of the land, references to race were all but eliminated from the text of the Georgia Constitution, state statutes, county codes, municipal ordinances, and policy and procedure manuals of government (and most corporate) entities. During this time, death sentencing and executions even realized a slower pace across the South.

Yet in some ways, surprisingly little institutional change has occurred since Jim Crow laws placed already-disadvantaged black Americans at an outrageous social, economic, and political handicap by advancing the wholesale separation of the races. Whereas in the past, a public official such as George Wallace could proclaim "segregation now, segregation tomorrow, segregation forever" during his inaugural address as governor of Alabama in 1963, white southerners are now apt to take symbolic political stands in defense of issues and emblems of their shared *heritage*, such as flying Confederate flags or protesting the removal of monuments dedicated to Lost Cause Confederate icons. In place of "white only" water fountains and seating areas, today there exists subtler segregation in the form of all-white private clubs and schools, gerrymandered legislative districts, upscale residential areas that effectively price out underprivileged populations, and a justice system that disproportionately harms people of color and the powerless. An abundance of research demonstrates that executions of black Americans bear close resemblance to lynching, if only because killing a white person, if one is black, increases the probability of a death sentence as much as sevenfold (Baldus, Pulaski, and Woodworth 1983). The resemblance is not merely cosmetic. Georgia realized more lynchings between 1882 and 1930 than any other state except Mississippi, thus explaining the historical continuity of disproportionately executing black offenders (see Litwack 1998). According to Randall Kennedy, the crux of the problem was "Southern whites' . . . unwillingness to recognize blacks' rights to protection against violence" in the decades following the Civil War (1997:39). All told, more than 100 antilynching bills were introduced in Congress from 1882 through 1951 (Holden-Smith 1995). Just three managed to pass the House of Representatives, and none survived Senate filibusters engineered by southern Democrats.

Although it was clear that delegates from the Deep South would combat any efforts to eliminate lynching through federal decree, the landmark Dyer Bill, which was defeated in 1922, succeeded in raising public awareness of the horrors of lynching and inspired numerous states to enact their own antilynching laws or strengthen already-existing legislation (*Chicago Defender* 1925). Lynching was on an inevitable decline despite the best efforts of southerners to protect their "national pastime" (*Chicago Defender* 1938b:3). Capital punishment, however, sustained itself through the early to mid-twentieth century as a substantive policy issue for proponents of de jure segregation (see figure 1.1). Since state-sanctioned executions were removed from public view and were the culmination of a legal case proceeding through the justice system—as opposed to the vigilante nature of lynch mobs—the resulting racial injustice was often less readily visible to northern politicians and liberal whites whose support had been essential to advancing the antilynching movement. Many simply perceived the problems of discrimination to be solved once the stark horror of lynching was no longer

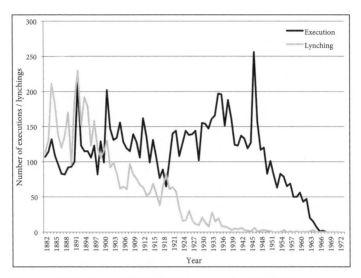

Figure 1.1. Executions and lynchings by year in the United States, 1882–1972. Source: Death Penalty Information Center 2017c; Tuskegee University Archives Repository 2010.

visible to them, meaning mob violence could be enveloped into the existing justice system and effectively accomplished inside the courtroom under the guise of law. With the resulting harms only affecting nonwhites and the poor, legal disenfranchisement via policing, judicial, and penal institutions could be propagated with broad social support among southerners whose focal concern was keeping blacks in their place and northerners who opposed lynching but lacked sufficient concern to pursue genuine equality.

Consider the framing of nine black teens in 1931 for the alleged rape of two white girls on a freight train, an incident that was described in the *Chicago Defender* as the attempted "lynching of innocent boys by a law court" (1931c:11). The case attained sufficient notoriety to prompt outrage among well-minded northerners (see *Chicago Defender* 1933; Thomas

1933) and even among Europeans who angrily stormed U.S. consulates and rioted at embassies in Germany and Switzerland (*Chicago Defender* 1931b, 1931c). Yet the ease with which the Scottsboro Boys and similarly situated black defendants could be "railroaded to the chair" (*Chicago Defender* 1931a:2) affirmed for many southern whites that criminal courts could properly dispense *justice* and compelled vigilantes in some jurisdictions "to curtail mob lynchings and wait for the 'legal lynching'" (*Chicago Defender* 1932:4; see also Clarke 1998). This shift away from lynching and toward state-sanctioned execution is what scholars refer to as the "substitution thesis" (that is, capital punishment replaced the fading practice of lynching as the primary means of subjugating blacks using targeted violence), and it was in many ways beneficial to states such as Georgia.[4] By 1937, 72 percent of voters and 57 percent of southern voters favored the passage of federal antilynching legislation (*Chicago Defender* 1937b). With opposition to lynching mounting and increasing pressure placed on southern legislators to curtail mob violence, the legal system offered a veneer of benevolence—in contrast to the visible physical brutality of lynching—to reaffirm the continued repression of blacks through institutionalized forms of social control.

The immediate solution was to stack juries with whites who were complicit with, approving of, or willing to ignore biased or blatantly unfair criminal proceedings against blacks. Table 1.1 indicates a considerable focus on the execution of nonwhites in the former Confederacy and other states with problematic records on race. Georgia ranks near the bottom, with 78 percent of its pre-*Furman* executions being nonwhites; all but two of the victims were white. The overrepresentation of black Americans is startling considering that by 1972, blacks represented only 11 percent of the total population. Using the courts to punish offenses

TABLE 1.1. Pre-*Furman* Executions in Southern States, 1945–1972

State	Total executed	Nonwhites	% nonwhites	Last execution
Alabama	44	33	75	1965
Arkansas	42	32	74	1964
Delaware	1	1	100	1946
Florida	83	56	67	1964
Georgia	152	119	78	1964
Kentucky	27	13	48	1961
Louisiana	45	32	71	1962
Maryland	21	17	81	1961
Mississippi	60	51	85	1964
Missouri	20	10	50	1964
North Carolina	72	59	79	1961
Oklahoma	18	3	11	1966
South Carolina	58	49	84	1962
Tennessee	25	16	64	1960
Texas	140	93	65	1964
Virginia	45	38	84	1962
Total	853	493	58%	

Source: Death Penalty Information Center 2017c.

against whites and correspondingly to minimize cases with black victims made the justice system a proxy for the lynch mobs of bygone days. As importantly, the thin veil of legal trappings surrounding black executions in the South was enough to satisfy disinterested whites who could no longer ignore the inhumanity of lynching but were effectively removed from the practical realities of injustice fostered by the rule of law.

Aside from the fleeting outrage in response to particularly egregious instances of courtroom discrimination, the vast majority of whites believed in the impartiality and fairness of the legal system. "Occasionally, a Scottsboro case awakens the lethargic North to a realization of what Southern 'justice' to the Negro means," wrote Raymond W. Logan in the *Chicago Defender*, "but then much more important events like the Hauptmann trial, the Saar plebiscite, or Miss Amelia Earhart's Pacific flight, quickly relegate the plight of the Southern Negro to the limbo from which he has momentarily impelled" (1935:10). With little political capital to be gained by either bigoted representatives from the South or disinterested northern officials, the welfare of economically and racially disadvantaged populations was not widely espoused: "[Politicians] have become a preferred class in sympathy with others who possess wealth. . . . Their opportunities and privileges precludes them from seeing and sympathizing with the common people" (*Chicago Defender* 1934:12). Consequently, the prevailing power structure of society effectively functioned to produce and reaffirm the larger cultural ideal that the legal system was capable of producing just and equitable outcomes in a far more humane manner than was being accomplished with lynch mobs (see McHoul and Grace 1993).

Using white-packed juries to rubber-stamp black executions became the preferred method, and for two decades, it worked rather well. By 1964, however, capital punishment had all but ceased, as the realization of botched executions had negatively impacted public opinion and political pressure from a strident civil rights movement made putting black Americans to death a risky proposition.[5] These developments empowered the first substantive legal challenge against capital punishment, as lawyers for the NAACP's Legal Defense Fund (LDF) charged that racism in the administration of the death penalty was reminiscent of lynching and Jim Crow–era discrimination.

The antilynching orientation was apparent in the early phase of the campaign, when the LDF took the Southern rape cases, for instance, *Maxwell v. Bishop*, in which black men were sentenced to death for the rape of white women. Such cases were part of an egregiously racist pattern in which the charge of capital rape was reserved for blacks. . . . Outside the South, rape was no longer a capital offense, and the decision-making of Southern juries made it plain that they regarded inter-racial sexual assaults as especially atrocious and infuriating. The echoes of the classic lynching scene were unmistakable. As the LDF's campaign developed, it broadened to challenge the death penalty in all its aspects—partly to serve its clients' interests, partly because the courts were proving unsympathetic to showings of racial bias, and partly because the lawyers came to regard capital punishment as an affront to civil rights that was inherently biased against unpopular minorities and the poor. (Garland 2010:218–219)

The LDF did succeed in getting the death sentence vacated in *Maxwell*, although the Supreme Court elected to avoid the issue of racial discrimination, instead ruling that an improper voir dire removed potential jurors simply because they expressed an opposition to capital punishment.

It was not until 1971 that the Supreme Court directly addressed the constitutionality of capital punishment, in *McGautha v. California*, deciding that a defendant's rights were not violated when the death penalty was imposed at the absolute discretion of a jury lacking any governing standards to guide its decision. In the companion case *Crampton v. Ohio*, the Court also upheld the constitutionality of a unitary trial wherein finding guilt and levying punishment occur in the same proceeding. David Garland notes that the Court's ruling in *McGautha* and *Crampton* seemed to "signal the end of abolitionists' hopes" because the majority chose "not to press further with the imposition of constitutional controls on state procedures in capital cases" (2010:224). In truth, though, it was clear following the Civil Rights Act of 1964 that the old ways of doing business, at least with regard to high-profile discrimination in social and economic practices, as well as in the administration of justice, were all but gone. If the subjugation of black Americans was to be continued in any sense, a new formula for controlling people of color had to be developed. Such a new policy had to eliminate the blatant bias attached to capital trials of black Americans— since newly registered black voters would be eligible for jury duty—by formulating a death penalty that involved a racially diverse body of eligible offenders.

Although it seems counterintuitive, the Supreme Court's march toward *Furman* was not necessarily unwelcome for states such as Georgia that needed an impetus to overhaul their death penalty statutes in accordance with a changing social, cultural, and racial climate in the post-civil-rights era. The High Court's ruling in *Furman v. Georgia* (1972) featured a three-way split that marked a distinct turn in direction from the unified liberal front that resulted in the drastic expansion of civil liberties under the stewardship of Chief Justice Earl Warren. Warren Burger, Harry Blackmun, William Rehnquist, and Lewis Powell were Nixon appointees; all voted against relief for William Henry Furman in support of capital punishment. Associate Justices Potter Stewart and Byron White, uncharacteristic of Kennedy appointees, voted for Furman but did so because both believed a better system of capital punishment was required and states should be trusted to come up with revised statutes that were fair and just. Associate Justice William Douglas joined Stewart and White in arguing that Georgia's death penalty *as applied at the time* was cruel and unusual because it was implemented in a discriminatory manner that targeted blacks and the poor. Only Associate Justices Thurgood Marshall and William Brennan were opposed to executions without caveat and advocated for their abolition. The existence of three divergent camps of opinion rendered the Court irresolute, divided, and unable to provide the constructive guidance needed to help legislators craft amended death penalty laws that would remedy the problem of racial bias.

The moratorium on executions imposed from the *Furman* decision gave southern states the political impetus to hammer out new, seemingly improved legislation, which 34 states did almost immediately following the *Furman* announcement in April 1972. Although the *Furman* ruling imposed a blanket commutation of all sentences of execution faced by prisoners, including notorious offenders such as Charles Manson, Richard Speck, and Sirhan Sirhan, across the country, death-row populations soon reached unprecedented levels as states passed new capital sentencing laws despite the reality that none of the convicted offenders could be legally executed. By the time the Supreme Court reassessed the constitutionality of capital punishment in *Gregg v. Georgia* (1976), there was a sense of urgency in many state houses to resume executions, even though the crisis was largely self-inflicted. When the Court put its stamp of approval on Georgia's revised process in *Gregg*, it established a template for any other state choosing to reinstitute capital punishment by introducing trial bifurcation into guilt and penalty phases, statutory aggravating (and mitigating) factors providing jurors necessary guidance "so as to minimize the risk of wholly arbitrary and capricious action" (*Gregg v. Georgia*, 428 U.S. 153, 189 (1976)), an automatic expedited appeal to the state supreme court, and the possibility for proportionality reviews to ensure that only the most appropriate cases yield a death sentence. Georgia legislators shrewdly chose to allay fears of discrimination by exploiting the nearly unregulated powers of respected circuit prosecutors in charging, penalty requests, and presentation of evidence in capital trials, backed up by judges standing for popular election or appointed in a best-man system with all the attributes of entrenched, well-connected southern whites in effect. The changes were deemed sufficient enough for Potter Stewart to conclude that "the concerns expressed in *Furman* that the penalty of death not be imposed in an arbitrary or capricious manner can be met by a carefully drafted statute that ensures that the sentencing authority is given adequate information and guidance" (*id.* at 195).

More than three decades later, the historical record clearly demonstrates that *Gregg* changed the shape of capital litigation in Georgia but has done little to eliminate the scourge of institutional discrimination perpetrated against blacks and other marginalized defendants, increasing the likelihood that prosecutors will seek execution in such cases, that juries will convict and sentence them to death, and that they may one day be exonerated for the crime that led them to being put on death row. The treatment of black Americans by the criminal justice system in Georgia is merely one aspect of a larger and historically momentous process that evolved in the time between the end of Reconstruction and Warren McCleskey's trek to the electric chair. In truth, the South had removed itself from any movement toward real egalitarianism, despite the pretense of progress toward universal equality in the decades preceding the Supreme Court's ruling in *McCleskey v. Kemp*. This reticence was not a matter of tacit resistance but one of systematic, reactionary sabotage employed against anyone, black or white, who supported an institutional remaking of southern society. The historian Eric

Foner laments, "the old view retains a remarkable hold on the popular imagination, including the pernicious idea, of which one hears echoes today, that expanding the rights and powers of blacks constitutes a punishment to whites" (2014:BR11). If Warren McCleskey had not already known this truth, he learned during his legal journey through the courts that the agents and vehicles of racial intimidation that were common during Jim Crow and through the civil rights movement still flowed across social and political institutions where structural discrimination could flourish under the guise of expanded racial equality.

2

Missed Opportunities on the Road to the Supreme Court

The respected and visionary legal scholar George Fletcher (2001) outlines a bilateral development of the U.S. Constitution following the Civil War, having serious ramifications for both legal philosophy and political life in the United States. On the one hand, a majority in the nation in the decades following the Civil War developed, albeit slowly, a national vision incorporating previously absent ideas of equality, fairness, and democracy. Fletcher regards the aura of Abraham Lincoln as the principal symbolic force in moving the republic from an objectified authority bound to and dependent on the popular will to a nation defined by its historical mission and humanitarian calling. Whereas the primary value of the American Revolution for the Founders was *freedom*—most recognizable as autonomy from the domination of the British Crown—there was a subsequent transition after the Civil War to an aim and value of *equality*. As importantly, Fletcher sees the highest power of the country evolving as well, from *the power of the living* to a concern for the nearly divine sway of history in our mission—a notion of the United States as a laudable, if not invincible, beacon of equality and democracy.

Of course, the state of Georgia and most of the former Confederacy held Lincoln in contempt. Hostile to any scintilla of parity with black Americans, southern whites continued to invoke arguments for pragmatic federalism and states' rights as a matter of tacit resistance. But such assertions were merely pretext to safeguard ongoing practices of systematic segregation and racial terrorism. The agents (e.g., Ku Klux Klan, Knights of the White Camelia) and vehicles of intimidation (e.g., church burnings, lynching, overt threats to black politicians, Black Codes) were common occurrences following Reconstruction, at the termination of both world wars, and across the span of Warren McCleskey's life, and they persevere on occasion even today. The U.S. South remains a symbolic battleground where the descendants of former slaves and people of color continue the struggle for equality in the face of stubborn and often violent resistance.

Gregg v. Georgia and the Institutionalization of Racial Intolerance

Although the segregationist tradition of overt racism was officially shunned following the sweeping victories of the civil rights movement, those southern whites opposed to reforms have defiantly permitted traditional racist ideology and the practice of discrimination to operate beneath a thin camouflage over social, cultural, and political institutions. The application of post-*Furman* capital punishment across the United States is no exception. In 1976, when the constitutionality of the death penalty was reaffirmed in *Gregg v. Georgia* (and companion cases *Jurek v. Texas* and *Proffitt v. Florida*), the Supreme Court assumed that the problem of discriminatory death sentencing would be cured through the introduction of four key features appended in Georgia's revised death penalty statute. The first is a bifurcated trial system, with the initial stage determining the defendant's guilt and the latter then used to ascertain an appropriate punishment. Second, the state provides a statutory list of aggravating (and mitigating, in most states) circumstances restricting the scope of cases for which death is an available sentencing option. During applicable trials, the judge instructs the jury that it must identify beyond a reasonable doubt the presence of at least one aggravator as supported by the evidence. If jurors accomplish this task, they then have the available option of issuing a death sentence or may select a lesser punishment.[1] Third, each case resulting in a death sentence is followed by an expedited, automatic, and mandatory appellate review by the state supreme court, which must include an assessment of the underlying conviction. Finally, Georgia proposed a review of capital sentencing proportionality whereby the state supreme court is required at regular intervals to evaluate each death sentence rendered in reference to similar cases throughout the state to confirm consistent application (see *Gregg*, 428 U.S. at 190–191, 196–198).

It is no surprise Justice Byron White wished to include a proportionality review in a landmark decision such as *Gregg*, in that he was a staunch advocate of safeguarding the Eighth Amendment's prohibition of cruel, inhumane, and unusual punishment (Stevens 2011). Yet in accepting at face value that Georgia's revised death process would eliminate or even sufficiently reduce the risk of capricious and arbitrary executions, the High Court essentially ruled that all of the potential sources of bias and error inherent in capital sentencing could be adequately addressed "by a carefully drafted statute that ensures [the jury] is given adequate information and guidance" pertaining to the "particularized nature of the crime and the particularized characteristics of the individual defendant" (*Gregg*, 428 U.S. at 195, 206). Such an inference is shocking in its naiveté. At the very least, the Court failed to consider how broader structural inequality in the justice system (racialized policing, prosecutors having unfettered discretion to decide when to seek capital punishment, and so forth) and larger society (such as poor and minority defendants being less likely to afford bail or have qualified legal representation) could precipitate disproportionate and discriminatory sentencing outcomes. Justice Marshall further charged that the American people are not sufficiently informed on the purposes and liabilities of capital punishment to draw reasonable conclusions about its consequences and effects (*Gregg*, 428 U.S. at 232), a fact that inevitably taints sentencing decisions. Even if we assume that most citizens are adequately knowledgeable about the nature and etiology of state-sanctioned executions, the Court's majority in *Gregg* simply presumed that judicial instructions to jurors, by way of identifying an aggravating circumstance beyond reasonable doubt, amounted to sufficient guidance in recommending a death sentence. *Guided discretion*, in its general form of balancing aggravation and mitigation, presupposes a universally consistent and proportionate application of capital punishment across all eligible homicide cases in a manner free of bias, racism, or any other extralegal considerations. It is a colossal expectation, and it failed in nearly every respect because distinct juries composed of disparate human beings cannot be expected to consistently and objectively apply aggravating factors in a case-by-case basis without being influenced (or, perhaps, *guided*) by their own biases, bigotry, and personal experiences.

Second, directing discrete guidance to the trial jury was in retrospect too little, too late. Any careful examination of the capital process immediately recognizes that the stages preceding the empanelling of a jury have heavy impact on the material, manner, and conduct of what a trier of fact will hear and eventually weigh, including investigations, prosecutorial charging decisions, evidentiary rulings, and sentencing requests. By focusing almost entirely on procedural guide-lines intended to remove prejudice from jury deliberations, the Supreme Court concluded in *Gregg* and *Jurek* that both Georgia's and Texas's revised statutes possessed sufficient safeguards to achieve super due process, which Margaret Radin defines as "a moral rationale that takes into account the existence of a political system and its fallibility" through enhanced substantive and procedural protections designed to minimize risk of error and ensure fairness in capital trials (1980:1183). Yet Potter Stewart's majority opinion is itself vague on details of how super due process could actually be achieved, noting only that "a small number of extreme cases" reflect "the continued utility and necessity of capital punishment in appropriate cases" (*Gregg*, 428 U.S. at 182).[2] Stewart, however, made no effort to define when a case was sufficiently (and objectively) extreme to merit execution as a proper sentence. We may logically conclude that such a threshold is reached when jurors definitely identify an aggravating circumstance. But this hardly stands as a rational process for detecting the worst-of-the-worst offenders or distinguishing the most extreme cases. At the very least, it places undue confidence in legislators' ability to codify the precise attributes whereby a particular homicide is so undeniably aggravated that an offender's death is the most suitable response and in the capacity of unique jurors to apply those aggravators across cases in a uniform manner yielding proportionate sentencing outcomes.

Providing a statutory list of aggravating circumstances may indeed supply guidance as to when capital punishment is an available sentencing option, but it in no way guarantees that aggravators are themselves reflective of the most death-worthy cases. In most weighing states, which require jurors to evaluate aggravation against the presence of any mitigating circumstances, as well as those that merely use a discrete list of statutory aggravators with no weighing requirement, committing a homicide for hire or to realize significant monetary gain amounts to an aggravating factor. Technically, any instance of a victim murdered by the beneficiary of the victim's life insurance would in effect be an aggravated homicide. It stands to reason that any homicide committed by a family member, business associate, or dependent of a victim would be subject to this sort of aggravation, whether or not it acted as motivation. In *Godfrey v. Georgia* (1980), for example, the petitioner, Robert Godfrey, was sentenced to death for slaying his wife and mother-in-law, on the basis of the statutory aggravator that his crime was "outrageously or wantonly vile, horrible or inhuman in that it involved torture, depravity of mind, or an aggravated battery to the victim" (446 U.S. 420, 422). The Supreme Court ultimately reversed his death sentence on the grounds that the aggravator used to justify his condemnation was unconstitutionally vague and therefore provided jurors with insufficient guidance. In fact, any homicide could potentially be deemed vile, horrible, or inhuman; and any murder can involve depravity of mind or aggravated battery. Yet eight years later, in *Maynard v. Cartwright* (1988), the High Court reversed course and wrote that an excessively vague aggravating factor can nonetheless be used to justify a death sentence if the state can sufficiently narrow its application to the case at hand. In other words, if a prosecutor can show that a circumstance common to a great many homicides, such as monetary gain, makes a specific case particularly vile, horrible, or inhumane, then the aggravator can nonetheless be lawfully applied.

If allowing for the consideration of unconstitutionally vague aggravating circumstances seems like a potential source of sentencing error, the problem is magnified when the death penalty is viewed as a moral response to crime. Potter Stewart makes this very point in *Gregg*: "Indeed, the decision that capital punishment may be the appropriate sanction in extreme cases is an expression of the community's belief that certain crimes are themselves so grievous an affront to humanity that the only adequate response may be the penalty of death" (428 U.S. at 184). Stewart's argument is both astounding and central to understanding Warren McCleskey's legal journey because it suggests that statutory lists of aggravating circumstances are not actually intended to identify the most appropriate or extreme cases but rather reflect a unifying communal likeness of belief—what Émile Durkheim ([1893] 1997) referred to as collective conscience— that certain crimes are a grave *affront to humanity*. Stewart's position effectively poses death sentencing as a subjective moral imperative rather than an objective legal response. In a constitutional sense, this is not per se problematic. The Supreme Court in *Lockett v. Ohio* (1978) established that capital punishment is legitimate when its use is morally appropriate (see Bilionis 1991). In *Lockett*, the majority ruled that capital statutes violate the Eighth and Fourteenth Amendments if they narrowly limit a jury "from considering, as a *mitigating factor*, any aspect of a defendant's character or record and any of the circumstances of the offense that the defendant proffers as a basis for a sentence less than death" (*Penry v. Lynaugh*, 492 U.S. 302, 317 (1989), emphasis in original). *Lockett* remains vital to the capital process because it "is the primary legal tool for ensuring that each decision to employ the death penalty is well grounded in morality" (Bilionis 1991:286).

Moral appropriateness in practice, however, has proven to be elusive (see Maratea 2016). Research suggests that there is no statistically evident correlation between a crime's egregiousness and death sentencing (see Donohue 2011). Capital punishment, then, is not reserved for the proverbial worst-of-the-worst offenders but rather is allocated according to the whims and wishes of prosecutors, who decide in what cases to seek death, and jurors, whose decisions in many cases have proven to be anything but morally appropriate. The result is a legal process whereby some offenders are sentenced to death for crimes deserving lesser punishment, while others are actually innocent of the crime for which they have been executed. Furthermore, U.S. courts have largely deemed it morally appropriate to execute the economically disadvantaged and nonwhites convicted of capital crimes against whites but are less enthusiastic when people of color are the victims.

The historical racialization of capital punishment notwithstanding, it is improper to condemn as racist those individuals who believe the death penalty is justified because it falls within the boundaries of their personal moral compass. Personal morality is shaped over the life course by a variety of social forces that extend beyond one's immediate family and close friends. Oftentimes, cultural narratives espoused by politicians, civic leaders, and professional journalists play a central role in molding perceptions about the death penalty. These accounts regularly simplify and misrepresent the conditions and consequences of state-sanctioned execution while blurring the ethical boundaries guiding the use and degree of punishment. In truth, most people confront executions only during high-profile murder cases when news reports convey the details of heinous crimes. Legislators, prosecutors, victims' families, and news reports often frame capital punishment as the only mechanism to achieve justice and closure (see Maratea 2016). By contrast, the public may also learn about death-row exonerations or when alleged offenders such as Troy Davis, Carlos De Luna, and Cameron Todd Willingham are put to death despite insufficient evidence to definitely confirm guilt. In these highly evocative moments—when vile offenders are facing execution or the wrongly convicted are absolved—the media tend "to cover the death penalty's popularity without caveats, limitations, or mention of support for alternative sentences" (Niven 2002:672). This sort of coverage not only tends to stoke outrage and provoke "public outcries for executions" (Vollum and Buffington-Vollum 2010:18) but also fails to contextualize the underlying moral and ethical dilemmas inherent to such a uniquely severe sanction.

It is fair to say that jurors in capital cases are never entirely removed from the social and cultural circumstances shaping their personal beliefs about punishment, justice, and race. Implementing a "carefully drafted statute" (*Gregg*, 428 U.S. at 195) cannot necessarily bridge the schism dividing personal notions of morality and emotion from reasoned critical analysis. Jurors, being human, do not cease being influenced by racial and other extralegal factors when determining guilt or deliberating a sentence. Even if one accepts statutory guidance as sufficient to remove the taint of racial bias from capital sentencing, it does nothing to stem police targeting the poor, the powerless, and people of color. Nor does guided discretion address the coercive sway of an outraged public or the unfettered power of prosecutors to disproportionately charge and seek death when confronted with cases involving black offenders and white victims. In reality, the more post-*Furman* capital statutes changed, the more capricious and arbitrary sentencing remained the same.

Déjà Vu All Over Again

Convinced that the application of capital punishment in Georgia following *Gregg* was no less capricious, arbitrary, and discriminatory than before *Furman* and following Warren McCleskey's failure to get his death sentence overturned by the Georgia state courts, the LDF, led by Jack Boger and Robert Stroup, began to take a more active role as the case headed toward federal litigation in 1981. Filing a writ of habeas corpus, LDF lawyers contended that racial discrimination could be proven via definitive statistical evidence of Georgia's disproportionate capital sentencing—most notably that black offenders and the assailants of white victims tended to be the most frequently sentenced to death. The foundation for the LDF's claims was a comprehensive statistical examination of Georgia homicide cases from the 1970s, the findings of which actually come from the cumulative result of two separate analyses conducted by the scholars David Baldus, Charles Pulaski, and George Woodworth of the University of Iowa. First is the Procedural and Reform Study (PRS), which used over 200 variables to evaluate 156 pre-*Furman* and 594 post-*Furman* defendants tried, convicted, and sentenced for murder in Georgia between March 1973 and July 1978. The PRS was an attempt to determine whether the "capital-sentencing system became more evenhanded in the post-*Furman* period" (Baldus, Woodworth, and Pulaski 1990:2). While the PRS was thorough in its analysis, "it lacked data on the strength of the evidence of the defendant's guilt, and, since it was restricted to murder convictions, it did not examine the possibility of pretrial discrimination in charging and plea bargaining" (Gross 2012:1912). In other words, the study was limited because it focused on only one phase of decision-making.

To fill the gaps missing in the PRS, the LDF commissioned the Charging and Sentencing Study (CSS), "with the expectation that the results might be used to challenge the constitutionality of Georgia's death-sentencing system as it has been applied since *Gregg v. Georgia*" (Baldus, Woodworth, and Pulaski 1990:44).[3] Covering the period from 1973 through 1979, the CSS was completed using a stratified random sample of 1,066 cases drawn from the 2,484 total defendants who were arrested and charged with homicide and subsequently convicted of murder or voluntary manslaughter; the data set was then statistically analyzed using more than 400 nonracial aggravating and mitigating variables. The goal of the CSS was to determine whether racial and other legally irrelevant factors influenced "the movement of cases through the system, which includes grand-jury indictment decisions, prosecutorial plea-bargaining decisions, jury guilt-trial decisions, prosecutorial decisions to seek a death penalty after the guilt trial, and jury penalty-trial sentencing decisions" (45).

The cumulative result of the PRS and CSS (hereafter referred to as the Baldus study) is an astonishingly thorough example of statistical analysis identifying a strong and consistent pattern of discrimination in capital sentencing applying not only to cases in Fulton County—the jurisdiction where Warren McCleskey was tried, convicted, and sentenced—but to the state of Georgia as a whole. Perhaps surprisingly, only 128 of the 2,484 eligible defendants (5.15 percent) were sentenced to death during the research period. Yet defendants convicted for killing a white victim received a death sentence 11 percent of the time (108 of 981 cases), as opposed to only 1 percent of those charged with murdering a black person (20 of 1,503 cases). As table 2.1 indicates, these disparities were primarily determined by *a race of victim effect*, whereby the assailants of whites get the death penalty at a much higher

TABLE 2.1. Cases in Which Prosecutor Sought the Death
Penalty and Capital Punishment Was Sentenced in Georgia, by
Race of Defendant and Victim, 1973–1979

Race of defendant	Race of victim	# of death sentences / total # of cases	% of cases for which prosecutor sought death	% of cases resulting in a death sentence
Black	White	50 / 233	70	22
White	White	58 / 748	32	8
White	Black	2 / 60	19	3
Black	Black	18 / 1,443	15	1

Source: Baldus et al. 1983.

rate than those who murder blacks do.[4] Also identified was
a secondary *race of offender effect*: black defendants were 1.1
times more likely to be sentenced to death, and the odds of
facing execution were 4.3 times greater for offenders accused
of murdering a white victim (Baldus, Pulaski, and Woodworth 1983). Furthermore, prosecutors were far more likely
to seek the death penalty when the victim was white and did
so 70 percent of the time when the offender was black (see
table 2.1). All told, the death penalty was meted out at a rate
8.3 times higher in cases with white victims than those with
black victims.

Of particular note, there was also an identified *case severity effect*, which means extralegal factors such as race did
not impact all cases equally. Race was actually less likely to
influence outcomes in high-range cases, where the crimes
were uniquely egregious (think of serial homicide or a mass
shooting), and in low-range cases, where there was the least
amount of aggravation. In midrange cases, however, the discrimination against black defendants and the discounting
of black victims were most pronounced. Because these trials generally involved interracial homicides, murders in the

commission of other felonies, and similarly situated crimes, they contained a complex amalgamation of aggravating and mitigating circumstances and consequently placed greater discretion in the hands of jurors or a judge when determining guilt and sentencing. Disproportionate outcomes in these cases became particularly pronounced when jurors directly associated aggravation and motive with race. Baldus and his colleagues concluded, "'Race hatred' really serves as a proxy for the defendant/victim racial combination, and it does so in a particularly virulent way. . . . The presence of a racially antagonistic motive increases the likelihood of a death sentence in white-victim case when, presumably, the defendant is black. By contrast, in black-victim cases, presumably with a white defendant, a 'race hatred' motive is a statistically significant mitigating circumstance" (1990:159). Simply put, being a black defendant, when all other variables are held constant, is in and of itself an aggravating factor, particularly when the victim is white. Hence, the best way to avoid execution is to murder someone who is not seen as white by prosecutors and jurors. In many respects, the Baldus study exposed Georgia's post-*Gregg* capital punishment system as one of the few post-segregation-era institutions in which unvarnished racist sentiments remained common parlance among whites who actually "become more supportive of the death penalty upon learning that it discriminates against blacks" (Peffley and Hurwitz 2007:996).

You Can Observe a Lot Just by Watching

If the NAACP had been unsure about using the Baldus study as the basis for challenging the constitutionality of Georgia's post-*Gregg* capital statute, all doubts were erased upon reviewing the definitive statistical findings of the CSS.

Although several Georgia capital defendants had already attempted to use the Baldus study as the basis for appealing their death sentences, each had stalled in the district courts when judges refused evidentiary hearings in their cases (see Kirchmeier 2015). It was not until Judge J. Owen Forrester of the United States District Court for the Northern District of Georgia allowed for an evidentiary hearing in McCleskey's case that the breakthrough was provided for LDF's lead counsel, Jack Boger, alongside Anthony Amsterdam, Vivian Berger, Julius Chambers, Timothy Ford, James Nabrit III, Deval Patrick, and Robert Stroup, to advance the claims of racial discrimination bolstered by the findings of the Baldus study. The central claim put forth by Boger was that Georgia law did not eradicate racism in its administration of capital sentencing despite the procedural remedies approved by the High Court in *Gregg*. Rather, the process remained effectively unchanged from the arbitrary, capricious, and discriminatory methods deemed unconstitutional in *Furman*.

In truth, several legal decisions during the 1980s helped to create a perfect storm that bolstered legal challenges to capital punishment and propelled *McCleskey* toward the Supreme Court. The first occurred in 1980, when the Court ruled in *Godfrey v. Georgia* that overly vague aggravating circumstances provide jurors with insufficient guidance because they fail to "provide a meaningful basis for distinguishing the few cases in which [the penalty] is imposed from the many cases in which it is not" (446 U.S. at 427). Drawing on precedent established in *Furman*, the Court determined that the failure to establish a "relevant" statutory aggravator resulted in capital punishment being arbitrarily applied in *Godfrey*, thereby violating the Eighth Amendment's "cruel and unusual punishment" clause (see Baldus, Woodworth, and Pulaski 1990:306).

The *Godfrey* decision proved important because it showed that the problems of capricious and arbitrary death sentencing remained present in Georgia after the reinstatement of executions in 1976, notwithstanding the Court's proclamation in *Gregg* that a carefully drafted statute would eliminate that very problem. Still, the LDF and McCleskey's appellate counsel likely knew that attacking Georgia's entire capital process on these grounds would result in failure because of "the lack of an acceptable standard for measuring excessiveness in an individual case and for challenging the constitutionality of an entire system" (Baldus, Woodworth, and Pulaski 1990:307). Barring clearly identifiable parameters by which an arbitrary sentence in one case could be used to generalize a systemic failure, any legal challenge would likely fall on unsympathetic judicial ears.

The same could not necessarily be said about legal challenges focused on sentencing proportionality and racial discrimination following the completion of the Baldus study. Such compelling statistical data could not easily be overlooked or discounted. Although the Supreme Court ruled in *Pulley v. Harris* (1984) that states are not constitutionally obligated to conduct a comparative proportionality review to determine statewide sentencing consistency, the suggestion that racial considerations provoke disproportionate sentencing outcomes stood in direct conflict with the Equal Protection Clause of the Fourteenth Amendment.

Since *Washington v. Davis* (1976) made plain that in order to prevail under an equal-protection claim a claimant must establish purposeful or intentional discrimination. It was unclear, however, whether an equal-protection claimant had to establish a "conscious" purpose or intent to discriminate, or whether evidence of a non-conscious, but identifiable re-

sponse to the racial characteristic of the cases would be sufficient. Finally, it was not clear whether proof of purposeful
discrimination in the system as a whole would be a sufficient
basis for granting a defendant relief if he were a member of
a disadvantaged minority. (Baldus, Woodworth, and Pulaski
1990:308)

Certainly the existence of racial bias had become more
difficult to detect in legal institutions following the eradica-
tion of Jim Crow and the social advancements of the civil
rights movement; and few people would suggest that by
1976, Georgia's revised capital statutes were drafted with the
manifest intent of executing blacks and other people of color.
At the same time, Anthony Amsterdam's argument for the
petitioner in *Jurek* takes on a foreboding tone when considering his warning that capital statutes very likely would work
differently than they appear on their face: "Death penalty
statutes are tidier in print than they are in operation . . . and
tidier now than they will be if they go for any period of time,
because of the natural tendency of any system to develop
shortcuts and outlets" (*Jurek v. Texas*, No. 75-5394 (oral arguments Mar. 30–31, 1976), at 10:50).

What Amsterdam meant by "shortcuts and outlets" was
not specified, although his subsequent writing on the operational dynamics of Georgia's capital statute in 1976 has
been very clear, in that the application of death sentencing
and the drift of criminal justice entities have tended toward
the old familiar ground of arbitrariness and capriciousness
(see Amsterdam 2007). It was Amsterdam's contention that
the definition of a capital crime, the "selective screening" of
death-eligible cases, and the array of available outlets to avoid
the use of capital punishment would be influenced "along
often intangible and impressionistic lines," thus permit-

ting "selective application [and] wholesale evasion" of death (*Jurek*, No. 75-5394, at 11:00).[5] In effect, Amsterdam was articulating the manner in which racialized—or perhaps even racist—outcomes could flourish in a supposedly sanitized and colorblind legal environment.

By the late 20th century, progress toward visible social equality and the movement toward race neutrality masked the fact that legal racial bifurcations had become hegemonic, meaning that they were accepted as status quo by the larger population and were self-reproducing to the benefit of white cultural authority, despite genuine legislative and judicial efforts to eliminate the very discrimination that was being germinated. Because political and legal structures function so effectively to protect those individuals and groups with money, status, and power—who happen to be disproportionately white—there is a certain inevitability to racial minorities, the economically poor, and other disenfranchised groups feeling the wrath of a justice system that does not equally safeguard all its citizens. This does not make the resulting outcomes (e.g., racially skewed prison populations) intentionally racist in a Ku Klux Klan, cross-burning sort of way. Rather, they are the product of structural or institutional racism that tends to permit the privileges that come with whiteness and disadvantages of color to endure over time (M. Alexander 2010; Delgado and Stefancic 2012; Vito and Higgins 2016).

"Structural racism" specifically refers to "the totality of ways in which societies foster racial discrimination through mutually reinforcing systems of housing, education, employment, earnings, benefits, credit, media, health care, and criminal justice" that "in turn reinforce discriminatory beliefs, values, and distribution of resources" (Bailey et al. 2017:1453). Unlike purposeful expressions of bigotry, such as someone proffering hate speech, structural racism perpetuates inequality through cultural imagery, social practices, and policy outcomes that occur "naturally, almost invisibly (and sometimes with genuinely benign intent), when it is embedded in the structure of a social system," tacitly reproducing the benefits of white privilege while systematically afflicting nonwhites in ways that are not necessarily evident to the unaffected (M. Alexander 2010:184; see also Lawrence et al. 2004; Vito and Higgins 2016). Michelle Alexander describes this type of racism as "a set of structural arrangements that locks a racially distinct group into a subordinate political, social, and economic position, effectively creating second-class citizenship," which reveals itself "not only in individual attitudes and stereotypes, but also in the basic structure of society" (2010:184–185).

In this way, structural racism can be thought of as a sort of laissez-faire bias that is more subtle than a lynching or the use of Black Codes (see T. Wilson 1965) and is often overlooked or flat-out disregarded as a real-world phenomenon by those who are not directly harmed by its effects. Yet, whether we are discussing racially disproportionate death sentences or the staggering infrequency with which police officers shoot unarmed affluent, white suburbanites as compared to urban black Americans, the use of statutory law has proven remarkably effective at maintaining a system of racial caste born from the vestiges of slavery, lynching, and Jim Crow segregation. Of course, not everyone argues that racially disproportionate outcomes are purposeful; even knowing "that race influences the decisions made by state's attorneys whether to seek or withdraw a capital charge does not mean that they are motivated by intentional racial prejudice or bigotry" (Paternoster et al. 2004:48). Part of the problem is that racial and socioeconomic disparities are often easy to overlook because most citizens generally trust legal authorities and institutions when they are not confronted with overt prejudice. To this point, psychological research indicates that "whites are more likely to empathize with and feel sympathy for other whites more than non-whites. White decision makers in the capital punishment system may, therefore, unconsciously make decisions that favor white victims. This greater sympathy for white victims by white decision makers may be particularly salient in intra-racial slayings, and certainly would characterize other decision makers besides state's attorneys" (Paternoster et al. 2004:49–50). This reality becomes even more striking when we consider how the courts interpreted statistical data on racial sentencing disparities in *McCleskey v. Kemp*.

Doubting Science

Regardless of whether Warren McCleskey knew it at the time, his ultimate fate might have already been sealed when district court and circuit court rulings effectively ignored powerful evidence that systemic and institutionalized discrimination produces legally disparate outcomes, even when racial bias is not the specific intent of law enforcement, prosecutors, or Georgia's overall death penalty process. Judicial skepticism about the usefulness of social science research in evaluating capital punishment was already apparent in lower court decisions before *McCleskey v. Kemp* ever reached the Supreme Court. In 1984, Judge J. Owen Forrester, in his district court opinion in *McCleskey v. Zant*, derided the Baldus study for having numerous faults, noting, "the data base has substantial flaws and . . . the petitioner has failed to establish by a preponderance of the evidence that it is essentially trustworthy" (580 F. Supp. at 360). In particular, Forrester condemned

what he described as coding errors, missing data on aggravating and mitigating circumstances, insufficient knowledge
about prosecutorial decision-making in capital cases, and the
presence of multicollinearity (see *id.* at 354, 356, 363), leading
him to conclude that the resulting data were "too inaccurate
to form a basis for useful conclusions; the statistical models
used by Baldus and his colleagues were flawed; the data did
not demonstrate that the capital-sentencing system in Georgia was discriminatory; and the statistical methodology used
had no value in this context" (Gross 2012:1913). Of note is the
district court's finding that "none of the models utilized by
the petitioner's experts are sufficiently predictive to support
an inference of discrimination" (*Zant*, 580 F. Supp. at 362).
Judge Forrester consequently ruled that Baldus's methodology failed to contribute anything useful to McCleskey's case
(*id.* at 372).

Nominated by President Ronald Reagan to a seat on the
United States District Court for the Northern District of
Georgia and confirmed by the U.S. Senate in December 1981,
Forrester was a relative neophyte on the federal bench when
he decided *McCleskey v. Zant*. Yet his assessment of the Baldus study was to have profound implications in setting the
tone for subsequent judicial rejections of the empirical evidence of discrimination evident in *McCleskey v. Kemp*. The
problem, however, is that Forrester may have lacked sufficient
comprehension of statistical analysis to reach an adequate
conclusion on the matter. In a rebuttal to Forrester's district
court decision, Baldus and his colleagues contended, "Judge
Forrester either misread the record or simply misunderstood
generally accepted standards of research methodology"
(Baldus, Woodworth, and Pulaski 1990:450). Samuel Gross
goes so far as to suggest, "most of the criticisms of Professor
Baldus' research are unfair and inaccurate, and many of the

statements about statistics are simply false" (2012:1913). Consider Forrester's assertion that multicollinearity gives reason to doubt the Baldus study's findings of bias in the Georgia capital system. Occurring when two or more independent (or predictor) variables in a logistical regression model may have a distorted relationship because they are highly correlated with each other, the incidence of multicollinearity, according to Forrester, "substantially diminishes the weight to be accorded to the circumstantial statistical evidence of racial disparity" identified in the Baldus study (*Zant*, 580 F. Supp. at 364; see also *McCleskey*, 753 F.2d 877). One must assume that Judge Forrester's apprehensions were concerned with the *predictive power* of the Baldus study's statistical models, namely, that the results demonstrating systematic bias in the harsh treatment of assailants of whites might be overstated or synthetic creations influenced by the existent multicollinearity. In asserting this point, the district court found that black-victim cases "are less aggravated and more mitigated than the white-victim cases disposed of in similar fashion" (*Zant*, 580 F. Supp. at 379), suggesting that the supposed race of victim effect identified by Baldus and his colleagues was actually a surrogate for some unaccounted-for aggravating circumstance primarily found in white-victim cases (see Finklestein and Levin 2001).

Forrester was presumably influenced by the state of Georgia's expert testimony from the statisticians Joseph Katz and Roger Burford, both of whom impugned the Baldus study on the basis that it did not adequately account for all of the factors and crime patterns that contribute to different sentencing outcomes. Katz and Burford also suggested that multicollinearity might have caused the regression coefficients to be inflated and to show more bias than actually existed. But neither Katz nor Buford clearly indicated the reasons he reached this conclusion or the tests he might have run to identify the problem. The statistical community commonly has used the Cox-Snell R^2 and the McFadden R^2 as diagnostic means to spot multicollinearity, to ensure that a given statistical model corresponds to the data being analyzed, and to determine if that model has high predictive power.[6] It is worth noting that the state of Georgia's statistical consultants did not specifically indicate which diagnostic tool they used to unearth the alleged condition of multicollinearity.[7] Such an indication would have helped to verify or rebut this concern, especially given Forrester's resolute finding that McCleskey "failed to make out a *prima facie* case of discrimination in sentencing based on either the race of victims or race of defendants" (*McCleskey*, 753 F.2d at 886).

Buttressing Forrester's methodological concerns was the district court's finding "that any racial variable is not determinant of who is going to receive the death penalty, and . . . that there is no support for a proposition that race has any effect in any single case" (*Zant*, 580 F. Supp. at 366). According to Forrester, statistical data such as those presented from the Baldus study might show *generalized* racial trends or disparities in outcomes but are unable to definitively indicate that race, in and of itself, tainted outcomes in any *specific* cases in a constitutionally impermissible manner. Because disparate results are perfectly legal if they are not proven to be caused by discriminatory factors, such as race, ethnicity, and sexual orientation, Forrester was able to conclude that "the best models which Baldus was able to devise which account to any significant degree for the major non-racial variables, including strength of evidence, produce no statistically significant evidence that race plays a part in either of those decisions [by prosecutors and juries] in the state of Georgia" (*Zant*, 580 F. Supp. at 368). The point was simple: statistical data only show differences in outcomes—that cases with black offenders and white victims yield more death sentences—but fail to confirm that racist or discriminatory intent was a catalyst in achieving those results. Forrester deferred to Katz's rather-questionable testimony that homicides of white victims by black offenders were consistently the most aggravated cases, and he therefore reasoned that without evidence of system-wide discrimination in Georgia, the Baldus study only indicated pervasive sentencing disparities and thus failed to show that racial considerations tainted McCleskey's specific case (*Zant*, 580 F. Supp. 338).

What becomes evident in the attendant language in Judge Forrester's district court opinion is that he acknowledged credible use of social science in a corroborative sense but at the same time denied that statistical inference can rise to the level of admissible evidence. Yet he had no apparent training in advanced quantitative analysis, and his opinion appears bereft of any understanding of research design and predictive value. According to Forrester, "The usefulness of statistics obviously depends upon what is attempted to be proved by them. If disparate impact is sought to be proved, statistics are more useful than if the causes of that impact must be proved. Where intent and motivation must be proved, the statistics have even less utility" (*McCleskey*, 753 F.2d at 888). Forrester's use of the word "proved" is problematic because inferential statistics allow a set of observations to be descriptively organized, modeled, and computed to test hypotheses and illustrate any possible cause-and-effect relationships between variables (that is, a change in variable A produces a corresponding change in variable B). This process affords the researcher an opportunity to draw conclusions from statistical analyses that are always expressed in terms of probability, reliability, and error.

The idea of proof conceived by Judge Forrester, as perhaps commensurate with the certainty of an eyewitness or the presence of a definitive motive, is not considered in statistical analysis. The Baldus study's finding that a white victim increased the probability of a death sentence for a black assailant by a factor of 4.3 is an expression of the predictive strength of the *race of the victim* variable as it acted on sentencing. This is not definitive proof of discrimination but statistical inference indicating a greater likelihood that Warren McCleskey received disparate treatment due to racialized patterns and practices systematically applied to black offenders. McCleskey's lead counsel, Jack Boger, referred to this exact point when he argued the state of Georgia had effectively instituted a bifurcated system of justice with very different outcomes for black and white offenders.

Black, White, and Gray All Over

Had Warren McCleskey been a job applicant instead of a death-row inmate, competing against a white applicant for employment with a state agency, and his treatment generated similar inferential evidence of discrimination, the state of Georgia would have been deemed liable under standards established a decade earlier in *Int'l Bhd. of Teamsters v. United States* (1977). In *Teamsters*, the Supreme Court explicitly noted that the individual plaintiff does not have to establish a prima facie case of disparate treatment, as was exacted in *McCleskey*, but can rely on statistical inference indicating a pattern of discrimination to show that there exists "a greater likelihood that any single decision was a component of the overall pattern" (431 U.S. 324, 359 n.45). Judge Forrester in his district court ruling effectively ignored *Teamsters* and chose to institute a separate, much higher, and decidedly unequal standard for offenders in capital cases. The decision was curiously paradoxical since the incidence of disparate treatment when the state is depriving a person of life would seemingly demand a standard that is at least equal to or even considerably lower than one used in diagnosing unfair hiring practices.

Although the Supreme Court later attempted to close this apparent conflictive void by insisting that capital decisions "are fundamentally different" and therefore unsuitable for statistical analysis (*McCleskey*, 481 U.S. at 294), the appellate process had already managed to severely restrict McCleskey's prospects for habeas corpus relief. Despite this fact and in spite of the district court's actions in discounting the Baldus study, Judge Forrester nonetheless overturned McCleskey's death sentence on the precedent established in *Giglio v. United States* (1972) that prosecutors must disclose to jurors any sentencing deals offered to witnesses in exchange for their testimony. By this time, Boger and Stroup had been investigating the circumstances of jailhouse informant Offie Evans's testimony for almost a decade. Both were skeptical that Evans, who was illiterate, almost perfectly transcribed his conversation with McCleskey, leading them to believe a recording device had been used. They also had suspicions about Evans's knowledge of details about the crime that had not been publicly released by the police, which Boger concluded was evidence of a working relationship between Evans and law enforcement (Simon 1995). Furthermore, Evans had contrived during his jailhouse conversation that he was related to Ben Wright, one of McCleskey's accomplices who was also present when Frank Schlatt was murdered, and "told McCleskey he had talked with Wright about the robbery and the murder" (*McCleskey v. Zant*, 499 U.S. 467, 474 (1991)).

Arguing to the district court that prosecutors retained Offie Evans as a jailhouse informant, Boger contended that the state subsequently failed to make the alleged statements elicited by Evans available to the defense and then neglected to properly notify the jury that Evans had been offered favorable treatment—and therefore had incentive to lie—in exchange for his testimony (see *Harvard Law Review* 1981). The Supreme Court of Georgia had previously acknowledged these infringements but insisted they were not key elements influencing McCleskey's eventual death sentence (see *McClesky v. State*, 245 Ga. 108, 112–113 (1980)). At the time, Evans had continued to deny being offered a deal; he claimed to reveal McCleskey's supposed confession only after an officer overheard the two and questioned him about the conversation. But Evans changed his tune during the district court proceedings, stating, "I wasn't promised nothing by [district attorney Russell Parker] but the Detective told me that he would—he said he was going to do it himself, speak a word for me" (Kirchmeier 2015:33). Taking into account the inconsistencies in Evans's version of events and the likelihood he might have lied on the stand, along with finding that jurors during McCleskey's original trial were not properly notified that Evans was offered a deal for his testimony, Judge Forrester determined that McCleskey's due process rights had been violated and therefore reversed his death sentence. Forrester ultimately concluded that Evans's testimony "was key evidence tying McCleskey to the homicide in a case based on non-substantial circumstantial evidence," and "the disclosure of the promise of favorable treatment and correction of other falsehoods in Evans' testimony could reasonably have affected the jury's verdict" (Kirchmeier 2015:34).

The decision to toss out McCleskey's death sentence despite Forrester's thorough rejection of the Baldus study was significant, as it called into serious question the legitimacy of McCleskey's underlying conviction. Although there is no compelling evidence to suggest McCleskey did not fire the bullet that killed Officer Schlatt, the presence of Offie Evans's undisclosed plea deal does suggest possible impropriety by the police and district attorney Russell Parker. None of this can be considered independent of the fact that the murder convictions of exonerated black defendants are 22 percent more likely to involve police misconduct than are white defendants' cases, and as a whole, black American prisoners who are found guilty of murder are about 50 percent more likely to be innocent than other convicted murderers (Gross, Possley, and Stephens 2017).[8] Regardless of whether Warren McCleskey was the actual gunman, several jurors from his original trial subsequently stated that they would not have sentenced McCleskey to death had they known Evans received a deal because "the whole issue about the actual murder came down to Offie Evans and the information they did not have about his bias" (Kirchmeier 2015:34).

All of these revelations about Offie Evans's testimony and the prosecutor's failure to properly disclose the plea deal to jurors notwithstanding, when *McCleskey* reached the Eleventh Circuit Court of Appeals, the presiding judges elected to reverse Forrester's *Giglio* decision and reinstate both McCleskey's conviction and death sentence on the premise that "speaking a word" on Evans's behalf did not constitute a deal sufficient to undermine his credibility as a witness and violate McCleskey's due process rights (see Kirchmeier 2015). The circuit court also chose to ignore Forrester's earlier district court ruling in *Zant* rejecting the value of statistical data. Rather than dismiss the Baldus study on methodological grounds, the circuit court acknowledged that the research sufficiently identified systemic disparities in Georgia's capital system but fell short of any constitutional threshold because it failed to identify any actual or purposeful discrimination.

> The district court held the [Baldus] study to be invalid. . . . We assume without deciding that the Baldus study is sufficient to show . . . that systematic and substantial disparities existed in the penalties imposed upon homicide defendants in Georgia based on race of the homicide victim, that the disparities existed at a less substantial rate in death sentencing based on race of defendants, and that the factors of race of the victim and defendant were at work in Fulton County. . . . Even if the statistical results are accepted as valid, the evidence fails to challenge successfully the constitutionality of the Georgia system. (*McCleskey*, 753 F.2d at 894–895)

Quite simply, the circuit court found that statistical data were insufficient to determine discriminatory intent in McCleskey's specific case as required by the Fourteenth Amendment and were further unable to meet the Eighth Amendment requirement to show irrationality, arbitrariness, and capriciousness in capital sentencing decisions (see Haines 1996; Patterson 1995).

The circuit court majority reasoned that even the most comprehensive statistical analysis merely indicates disparities in outcome, which, however acute, cannot be conclusively proven to result from purposeful prejudice or racist provocation on the part of the state or any institutional actors (judge, jurors, prosecutors, and so forth) in a given case. It was not contended by the court that discrimination does not exist and is not affecting outcomes in capital cases, but instead the magnitude of bias identified by Baldus was insufficient to meet whatever constitutional level is necessary to challenge the application of capital punishment in Georgia. While it is true that empirical data may indicate systematic disparities in capital sentencing without definitely proving that those discrepancies occurred due to any prejudicial actions, the court's rationale is nonetheless perplexing for a few reasons. First, by portraying statistical research as immaterial to understanding the dynamics of capital sentencing, the only way petitioners can meet the resulting burden of proof is in the unlikely event that individuals involved in their cases choose to publicly identify themselves as bigots who deliberately tainted a case with racial bias. On this matter, the Eleventh Circuit Court of Appeals concurred with Judge Forrester's earlier district court ruling, which held that the plaintiff's burden was to show race played a part in "either the decision of the prosecutor or the jury" and that statistical evidence of system-wide disparities was "incapable of saying whether or not any factor had a role in the decisions to impose the death penalty in any particular case" (Baldus, Woodworth, and Pulaski 1990:341).

Second, the circuit court chose to discount the implications of the Baldus study's most compelling statistical model showing that on average a white-victim crime is 6 percent more likely to yield a death sentence than analogous black-victim crimes (*McCleskey*, 753 F.2d at 896–897). Gross notes that "six percent may not seem like a lot in some contexts—say the difference between male and female employment at a plant with 53% men and 47% women," but when considered "in the context of capital sentencing in Georgia in the 1970s, a good description of the '6%' racial disparity found by Baldus (after controlling for many other variables) is that it corresponds to an increase in the probability of a death sentence from 3% to 9%" (2012:1914). It may very well be that the circuit court judges deemed that 6 percent figure to be too small to merit consideration. Or perhaps they simply determined that it was constitutionally insignificant since there was no clear evidence that the identified disparity was caused by discriminatory intent.

The More Things Change, the More They Stay the Same

In order to understand why the circuit court would overlook such stark racial contrasts in Georgia death sentences unearthed by the Baldus study, given the state's historical treatment of nonwhites, it is useful to consider whether the social advancements toward racial equality of the past half century made any significant changes in Georgia's criminal justice system. Some social scientists (mostly criminologists and sociologists) argue that the cultural transformations brought about by the civil rights movement were not really successes, or even entirely reformatory, but merely transitions to, and adaptations of, newer forms of subordination intended to stigmatize and control black Americans (Wacquant 2001; M. Alexander 2010). Loïc Wacquant sees a succession of *peculiar institutions*—from slavery to Jim Crow, then ghetto segregation, and now the prison system—as "kindred *institutions of forced confinement* entrusted with enclosing" blacks and neutralizing "the material and/or symbolic threat" they pose to white civil society (2000:377, emphasis in original). More recent research on stop-and-frisk, stand your ground, racial profiling, and the overrepresentation of black Americans in the ranks of convicts and ex-convicts seems to confirm Wacquant's point and align with the sentencing disparities revealed by the Baldus study.

Michelle Alexander (2010) and Michael Tonry (2011) largely agree with Wacquant's assertions on the effects of mass incarceration and the justice system's disfranchise-

ment of nonwhites. Both insist that racial caste and the in-
struments of oppression have merely been reshaped to allow
mainstream America to once again close its collective eyes
to discrimination. It is from this hegemonic nexus of contemporary criminal justice policy extending from the rise
of Reagan-era tough-on-crime and law-and-order strategies
that the most highly symbolic sanction of capital punishment
bears an eerie resemblance to lynching.[9] This perspective is
affirmed in a report from the Equal Justice Initiative (2015)
that documents approximately 4,000 southern lynchings between 1877 and 1950, from which researchers conclude that
"the threat of death by lynching was far more influential in
shaping present-day racial reality than contemporary Americans typically understand." In this sense, lynching was the
predecessor of racial animus in the contemporary criminal
justice system and "declined as a mechanism of social control
as the Southern states shifted to a capital punishment strategy, in which blacks began more frequently to be executed
after expedited trials" (*New York Times* 2015; see also Equal
Justice Initiative 2015).

The reasons for this shift can be traced back to the 1930s,
when a substantial number of Americans—including prominent southerners—had become increasingly uncomfortable
with the barbarism of public lynching. Mounting social disdain of barbaric lynch mobs precipitated its eventual extinction. Vigilantes soon began to employ more discreet tactics:
"Instead of a large, noisy mob, a small group of five or six
persons now kidnaps the victim and maim or kill him." These
"unpublicized lynchings" often went unreported, creating the
perception that lynching was dying out (*Chicago Defender*
1940b:1), when in reality mobs had merely been replaced by
surreptitious posses. This evolution toward covert lynching
tactics was little more than a clandestine mechanism allow-

ing the subjugation of blacks to remain intact (see Woolfolk 1938). It also reflected that vigilantism and racially bifurcated justice were not confined to the spectacle of public lynching but rather were infused throughout the existing justice system. The veil of justice perpetrated by the legal system operated with the pretense of due process yet sufficiently protected white superiority in a more hidden and legally accepted manner than was being accomplished via lynch mobs. Many infamous cases, such as the Scottsboro Boys, George Stinney, and even the railroading of immigrants such as Sacco and Vanzetti in the North, came to reflect this fundamental shift toward a thinly veiled state-sanctioned system of legal lynching, echoed by all-white, male juries and legitimated by criminal courts. But there is no mistaking that racialized authority constituted inside courtrooms and behind prison walls under the veneer of law was eerily "reminiscent of the power exercised in the old system" of lynching (Foucault [1977] 1995:129).

According to the legal scholar William Graham Sumner, understanding the transference from lynching to mass incarceration and capital punishment and why their intrinsic association is misunderstood by many Americans stems from the fact that "law is a dependent variable determined and shaped by current mores and the opinion of society" (Sumner 1906, quoted in Zimring and Hawkins 1971:34). For a considerable percentage of the population, current laws criminalizing the discriminatory treatment of nonwhites, women, immigrants, the LGBTQ community, and certain cultural nonconformists are entirely out of step with privately held opinions. In the state of Georgia and throughout the United States, second-class citizenship for black Americans as a time-honored and customary practice is a persistent remainder of Old South traditions, as much as Confederate battle flags, images of

Robert E. Lee, and even the color gray. When considering the theoretical supposition posed by Wacquant, Alexander, and Tonry that social institutions function to suppress and exploit people of color, it follows that the moratorium on capital punishment initiated by *Furman* and the many post-*Gregg* reforms, including guided discretion and narrowing of the class of offenses and offenders eligible for capital punishment, are merely changing attributes of a continuing effort to subordinate black Americans. In many ways, as capital punishment continued to evolve in states such as Georgia, it never really changed at all. Cloaked in a guise of humanism, the use of statutory law effectively maintained a system of racial caste that preserved a culture of white authority in a world without slavery, convict-lease, or widespread lynching. Faced with this reality, it became abundantly clear when *McCleskey v. Kemp* reached the United States Supreme Court that the majority of justices would do little more than turn a blind eye.

3

Black Murders Are *Different*

In the fall of 1986, Warren McCleskey's legal team successfully petitioned for a writ of certiorari asking the Supreme
Court to reconsider the circuit court decision allowing
the state of Georgia's death warrant to go unhindered. By
this time, the Baldus study had become widely recognized
as landmark research in sentencing proportionality, and
the Supreme Court's decision to review *McCleskey* set off
a wave of similar discrimination claims that moved the
Court to consider granting stays of execution in a number
of similar cases until *McCleskey* was heard and ruled on
(Wrightsman 1999). In one such case, *Rook v. Rice* (1986),
the petitioner, John William Rook, intended to present
statistical research conducted by the University of North
Carolina professors Barry Nakell and Kenneth Hardy as evidence of systemic racial disparities in North Carolina capital
sentencing similar to those identified in *McCleskey*. Nakell
and Hardy (1987) argue in their analysis that the phras-
ing "arbitrary and capricious" has applicable definitions,
in that discrimination explicitly includes invidious factors
influencing eventual sentencing decisions, while arbitrariness offers a description of outcomes uncontrolled by any
discernable standards, namely, the Eighth Amendment's
safeguard against cruel and unusual punishment. Discrimination therefore becomes an important consideration since
the constitutionality of a law that appears neutral on its face
demands a plaintiff demonstrate that its administration was

an intentional violation of the Equal Protection Clause of the Fourteenth Amendment.

This point is profound in its implications. After all, post-*Gregg* death penalty statutes were drafted as race neutral and with the intention of being applied uniformly; that is, all defendants facing the possibility of death are to be afforded the same bifurcated trial procedure, statutory guidance for when juries may select death as a sentencing option, an expedited appellate review, and, in theory, a proportionality review to ensure only the worst-of-the-worst offenders are being sent to death row. In practice, however, the capital process is necessarily implemented by fallible humans and embedded within a larger criminal justice system that has always been plagued by problems of misconduct, bias, discrimination, subjective decision-making, and an overall lack of uniformity in treatment often on the basis of legally irrelevant factors such as race, ethnicity, social class, and gender. In other words, it hardly matters that statutes governing capital punishment are intended to function in a neutral manner if arbitrariness or discriminatory treatment infect the justice system from the first moment of police contact, in prosecutors' judgments to seek death, or a jury's decision to condemn a defendant.

The Supreme Court eventually denied Rook's petition despite strong opposition from Justices Brennan and Marshall, who argued that a stay of execution should have been granted given Rook's presentation of statistical data demonstrating discrimination in capital cases that so closely mirrored the evidence already before the Court in *McCleskey v. Kemp*.[1] Both Brennan and Marshall had established in *Furman* their belief that capital punishment was unconstitutional in all circumstances. Brennan specifically articulated four principles by which the death penalty can be established as cruel and unusual. First, he argued that executions are so extreme in their severity and finality that they degrade human dignity since the condemned effectively lose their *right to have rights*. Because capital punishment is irrevocable, executed offenders have no opportunity for redemption and are thus denied their basic humanity. Second, Brennan suggested that capital punishment "is tolerated only because of its disuse" (*Furman v Georgia*, 408 U.S. 238, 300 (1972)). By this, he meant if states have legal authority to execute deserving offenders but rarely do so, then it is clear that society has considerable reservations about the death penalty. Third, executions were deemed unnecessary because the "punishment cannot be shown to be serving any penal purpose that could not be served equally well by some less severe punishment" (*id.* at 300). In arguing that the death penalty is neither a deterrent nor needed for the protection of society—in that there is no evidence of more crime or vigilantism in non-death-penalty jurisdictions—Brennan concluded that imprisonment was a sufficient sanction, thereby rendering executions excessive and unconstitutional. Finally, the issue of arbitrary infliction of punishment was addressed in relation to usage of the death penalty being "freakishly" or "spectacularly rare" (*id.* at 293). Whereas lawyers for Georgia had argued in *Furman* that a small number of the most appropriate *worst-of-the-worst* offenders were executed due to the state's practice of informed selectivity (taking proper steps to ensure that only the most deserving are executed), Brennan countered by claiming that Georgia's capital process was tantamount to a lottery (*id.* at 293). His reasoning was that no party had identified a rational basis for differentiating the small number of offenders sent to death row from the much-larger majority given prison sentences. Of course, as the Baldus study eventually proved, the differentiation between prison and death is primarily related to matters of race, gender, and social class, not the severity of the crime.

The Deadly Summer of 1987 in Louisiana

For both Brennan and Marshall, the prevalence of cases being petitioned to the Supreme Court by the middle of the 1980s, alongside newly discovered statistical evidence of systemic racial disparities in statewide death sentencing practices, validated that their majority opinions in *Furman* had always been correct. Notwithstanding the High Court's refusal to hold the petition for certiorari in Rook's case, stays were granted in several others pending the outcome of *McCleskey*, with the ripple effect being most prominently felt in Louisiana, where executions were stayed in *Wingo v. Blackburn* (1986), *Watson v. Blackburn* (1986), *Glass v. Blackburn* (1986), *Moore v. Blackburn* (1986), *Borgdon v. Blackburn* (1986), and *Rault v. Blackburn* (1986). In *Wingo*, the plaintiff alleged that death sentencing in Louisiana was applied in a racially disproportionate and arbitrary manner in the incidence of a white victim. Upon review of the case, the Louisiana Supreme Court concluded that the "argument that there is a racial component raises no cognizable claim" (783 F.2d 1046, 1052), citing *Moore v. Maggio* (1984) as precedent.[2] Similarly, in *Watson v. Blackburn*, the victim, Kathy Newman, was abducted, raped, and murdered on April 5, 1981, by the African American defendant Willie Watson. Even though Watson confessed to the crimes and was sentenced to death two months later, his attorneys insisted that some death-qualified[3] jurors were excluded in order to facilitate his condemnation. Along with expressing concerns about a litany of other alleged trial irregularities, the attorneys also argued that the aggravating factor of a significant prior criminal history used to secure

TABLE 3.1. Louisiana Executions in 1987

Execution date	Name of offender	Age of offender	Sex of offender	Race of offender	Age of victim(s)	Race of victim(s)	Sex of victim(s)
June 7	Benjamin Berry	31	Male	White	37	White	Male
June 9	Alvin Moore	27	Male	Black	23	White	Female
June 12	Jimmy Glass	25	Male	White	55, 51	White	Female, male
June 16	Jimmy Wingo	35	Male	White	55, 51	White	Female, male
July 20	Willie Celestine	30	Male	Black	81	White	Female
July 24	Willie Watson	31	Male	Black	25	White	Female
July 30	John Brogdon	25	Male	White	11	White	Female
August 24	Sterling Rault	36	Male	White	23	White	Female

Watson's death sentence was unconstitutionally vague. When the case reached the Fifth Circuit Court of Appeals, Watson's cert application was curtly denied because the majority judges found meritless the "claim of discrimination in the imposition of the death penalty on blacks who murder whites" (*Watson v. Blackburn*, 798 F.2d 872, 872 (1986)).

Altogether, there were eight executions in Louisiana during the summer of 1987 (see table 3.1), a staggering tally considering that only seven executions had been conducted in the preceding decade following the state's reintroduction of the death penalty in 1977. On the surface, the appellate courts in Louisiana, the Fifth Circuit Court of Appeals, and even the U.S. Supreme Court saw little merit in any of these individual cases. Taken as a whole, however, they presented some common elements indicating a pattern and practice of racial and gendered victim-based discrimination comparable to what the Baldus study found in Georgia.[4] Presumably, it was not lost on the sitting justices that the Supreme Court was suddenly faced with a litany of petitioners contending prejudiced death sentencing and that those cases bore at least a slight resemblance to *McCleskey*, specifically in regard to victim bias. Any decision by the Court acknowledging or even marginally conceding the problem of arbitrary and racialized death sentencing threatened the entire structure of capital punishment reform put in place by *Gregg, Proffitt*, and *Jurek*. Such an outcome not only would strike a decisive and fatal blow to the constitutionality of executions in the United States but would also call into question the operational legitimacy of the entire justice system. After all, if the penal sanctions in cases presumably involving the worst offenders and harshest sanctions are flawed, there is no way of guaranteeing that the punishments given to lower-level offenders for more trivial crimes are any less fallible and free of bias.

Moving Forward in Reverse

Despite repeated losses in the lower courts, the sheer importance of *McCleskey* in using statistical data to address the role of race in capital punishment and the functioning of the entire justice system, more generally, should have been difficult for the Supreme Court to ignore. Still, five of the Court's justices initially voted against accepting the case for review. However, because of the Court's unofficial tradition of taking cases if four justices vote to hear them (Harry Blackmun, William Brennan, Thurgood Marshall, and John Paul Stevens), *McCleskey* was formally granted a petition for certiorari in July 1986, assuring that the case would be heard before the Supreme Court. Jack Boger was cautiously optimistic that the Court would recognize the validity of the empirical data presented from the Baldus study and rule in favor of McCleskey (Kirchmeier 2015), but he also knew that five justices had already voted against granting the writ of certiorari notwithstanding that the entire petition was based on statistical evidence indicating profound sentencing discrimination. The task in front of Boger therefore required that he convince at least one justice to flip sides.

In retrospect, the fate of Warren McCleskey and the assessed credibility of capital sentencing throughout the criminal justice system hinged on the swing vote of Associate Justice Lewis Powell. A child of privilege born in the tidewater region of historic Hampton Roads, Virginia, Powell was described in the *New York Times* as "a patrician son of the Old South" (Greenhouse 2002). Having earned law degrees from Washington and Lee University (1931) and Harvard Law School (1932), Powell cultivated a reputation as a highly regarded corporate lawyer who represented the tobacco industry and spent nearly a decade on the board of directors of Philip Morris prior to his nomination to the Supreme Court. An ardent anticommunist and stalwart member of the Democratic Party, Powell had directly confronted the effects of discrimination while chairman of the Richmond (Virginia) school board from 1952 to 1961, when there was considerable organized resistance to desegregation efforts.[5] As president of the American Bar Association (ABA), he also advocated support for federal-government programs to provide legal services for the poor.

Given Powell's background and life history, he was undoubtedly aware of the historical legacy of racial inequality and intolerance in Georgia and throughout the Deep South. At the very least, he had no reason to doubt the Baldus study or the oral arguments that would be presented to the Court by Jack Boger in *McCleskey v. Kemp*. Powell was an enigmatic justice, however. Nominated to the Supreme Court by Richard Nixon in 1971—having previously turned down Nixon's first request in 1969—Powell was certainly a judicial conservative but also had a reputation for occasionally working with his more progressive colleagues. Powell sided with the majority to legalize abortion in *Roe v. Wade* (1973) and provided the swing vote in many cases when the Court was particularly divided. But he had dissented against the abolition of capital punishment in *Furman* and supported reinstating executions in *Gregg*, albeit while concurring with the majority in striking down the death penalty for rape in *Coker v. Georgia* (1977).[6] Powell also sat attentively in judgment and wrote copiously on cases of employment discrimination involving empirical statistical evidence. In *McDonnell Douglas Corp. v. Green* (1973), Powell wrote for a unanimous majority establishing that a plaintiff must be afforded an opportunity to present facts to show an inference of discrimination. It was Powell's opinion in *McDonnell Douglas* that set out a framework for disparate treatment in employment discrimination cases; it remains a recognized precedent. If Powell had accepted the validity of statistical data showing the influence of race on employment decisions, then Boger had every reason to believe he might do the same when faced with overwhelming empirical evidence that race affects death penalty sentencing decisions.

Powell's centrist nature notwithstanding, by 1987 the Supreme Court's composition leaned decidedly to the right. Sandra Day O'Connor had been appointed to the Court in 1981, replacing the outgoing Potter Stewart, who had expressed moral opposition to capital punishment and alongside Byron White formed the vital swing votes in *Furman* (see Mandery 2013). Stewart was very much a judicial moderate, even though he sometimes aligned with justices on the right. With the appointment of O'Connor, however, conservatives held sway on the Court. The decade also saw Chief Justice Warren Burger announce his retirement, effective at the end of the 1986 term. President Reagan appointed Associate Justice William Rehnquist as his replacement. Richard Nixon's last appointee to the Supreme Court in 1972, Rehnquist's principal qualification was his reputation for concise, logical decision-making based in *legal positivism* (see S. Davis 1986). He also had a keen sense of integrity for an unemotional judiciary that sparingly intervened in the business of the states. Rehnquist's deep respect for states' rights and narrow reading of the law, together with his icy demeanor during Court sessions, made him a frequent target of liberal critics. Judicial colleagues never shared those indictments of Rehnquist as frigid, dismissive, and elitist, having known his sharp sense of humor and affable personality (see Savage 1992).

With O'Connor's appointment and Rehnquist's ascendency to chief justice, Reagan had a Court sympathetic to his law-and-order approach to combating crime; the mass warehousing of prison inmates during the 1980s replaced any semblance of corrections aimed at rehabilitating inmates. Judicial discretion was eliminated in favor of harsh mandatory minimums and punitive punishments such as three-strikes laws and "scared straight" programs, which were believed to have a deterrent effect. Of course, all of these policies in their enforcement were targeted at racial minorities and the poor, a fact that became particularly pronounced in light of the devastating consequences caused by the War on Drugs in the black American community. Nonetheless, further support for this agenda was solidified during the final years of Reagan's second term, when Warren Burger's retirement elevated Rehnquist to chief justice and left an opening for Antonin Scalia to be appointed from the prestigious District of Columbia Circuit Court of Appeals. Scalia was a well-known law professor at the University of Virginia and University of Chicago who had served intermittently in minor positions in the Nixon and Ford administrations, working up to assistant attorney general for the Office of Legal Counsel in 1974. He had a reputation as a rock-ribbed Republican and brilliant student, coming to the profession via Georgetown University and Harvard Law School, the latter summa cum laude. Scalia was a founding member of the conservative Federalist Society, and his vocal positions in support of executive privilege and in opposition to abortion on demand, as well as his strict constructionist legal philosophy, made him rising star among Republicans advocating far-right politics.

Two possible candidates for Rehnquist's vacated associate justice post had initially emerged; they were Scalia and the Yale law professor Robert Bork, who had previously served as a federal appellate court judge for the District of Columbia. Bork was well known from his time as solicitor general in the Nixon administration, when at the president's behest, he fired special prosecutor Archibald Cox while he was investigating the Watergate scandal. He was also recognized for his brilliant legal writing and inherently conservative views, which were as celebrated among Republicans as they were notorious among Democrats. A lightning rod for liberal allegations, Bork was condemned by critics for wanting to turn the clock back on civil rights and reverse *Roe v. Wade*. Liberal backlash alongside the political baggage picked up in the Watergate affair, when the Justice Department split apart over Nixon's misuse of executive privilege, steered the Reagan administration toward Antonin Scalia, in hopes of avoiding a protracted battle in the Senate. The decision proved correct, as the Senate swiftly voted to confirm Scalia by a 98–0 vote.[7] At the time of Scalia's nomination and swearing in just weeks before the Court was scheduled to hear *McCleskey*, little was known of how he would interpret both the matter of executions and the Baldus study; he had never presided over a death penalty case while at the circuit court (see Kirchmeier 2015). However, in subsequent years, Scalia's unequivocal support of capital punishment became clear; he went so far as to express the view that conclusive evidence of actual innocence might be ignored if a condemned defendant's legal process has been properly fulfilled since the Constitution does not necessarily preclude states from executing the innocent (*Herrera v. Collins* (1993); *In re Davis* (2009)).

McCleskey v. Kemp Reaches the Supreme Court

With Scalia in place as the newest associate justice, the full Court was ready for the presentation of oral arguments in *McCleskey v. Kemp* on October 15, 1986. The opening statement of Jack Boger, McCleskey's attorney, focused on Georgia's history of racially bifurcated law enforcement dating back to before the Civil War. Although Boger insisted that the ratification of the Fourteenth Amendment halted some of the openly racist state-sanctioned practices of bygone days, he underscored the persistence of discriminatory attitudes in the minds of prosecutors and jurors who inject "racial considerations [into] Georgia's sentencing system" (*McCleskey*, No. 84-6811, at 2:01). Boger buttressed this assertion with a robust defense of the statistical methods and findings of the Baldus study, which had been so sharply criticized by Judge Forrester in his earlier district court ruling. Boger not only reminded the Court that the killers of whites were sentenced to death at roughly 11 times the rate of those who assail black victims but also pointed out that the source of those data came directly from the Georgia Pardons and Parole Board and the state's supreme court. When questioned by Byron White about the use of trained law school students and graduates to code and interpret research data, Boger rejected

Forrester's rebuke of the methodological practices used in the Baldus study, claiming that the lower court had reached an erroneous conclusion (*McCleskey*, No. 84-6811, at 7:26–10:01).

Defending the Baldus study's integrity was actually of secondary concern to Boger since the Court assumed its validity and did not necessarily share Forrester's cynical view of statistical research (*McCleskey*, 481 U.S. at 291 n.7). Most of the substantive questions posed to Boger focused on whether the Baldus study indicated that McCleskey was specifically harmed by acts of intentional prejudice. Noting that discrimination could be deduced from the available statistical evidence of statewide racial disparities, Boger took a leap of faith that the Court would recognize that the comprehensiveness of the Baldus study verified that those capital sentencing discrepancies could not be explained by anything other than racial bias. The problem facing Boger stemmed from the fact that the statistical data offered in the Baldus study were unable to conclusively *prove* that race enters into every capital sentencing decision or even McCleskey's particular case. In truth, inferential statistics only illustrate relationships between variables, in this case race and sentencing; they do not speak specifically to causality with sufficient precision to determine whether and how race played a specific role in McCleskey being sentenced to death. This is precisely why Boger argued that capital punishment in Georgia was so overwhelmingly racialized that prosecutorial decisions and jury deliberations were unavoidably imbued with racial animus regardless of whether any individual case was purposely sullied. Justices O'Connor and Rehnquist continued to press the issue, asking Boger whether he was obliged to show discriminatory intent on the part of actors in McCleskey's specific trial. Boger conceded that juries deliberate in secret and prosecutors are not required to disclose their reasons for pursuing capital punishment, meaning that the precise reasons for why death is sought or chosen as the appropriate sentence in any given case can only be inferred from the Baldus study's data.

Scalia shifted to questioning away from establishing proof of intentional discrimination and sought to discern the parameters of legal protections based on physical characteristics, asking Boger whether it should be unlawful to "convict people more readily because they are ugly, or because they are shifty-eyed." Boger rebuffed the comparison, noting that the Court has not "afforded the same kind of protection, constitutionally, to shifty-eyedness" or being physically unattractive (*McCleskey*, No. 84-6811, at 23:56).[8] O'Connor soon followed by addressing the issue of discretion and whether racial bias meaningfully affects capital punishment because juries have the ability to sentence defendants to death or a lesser punishment such as long-term imprisonment. The query was one of present-day practicality and largely diverged from Boger's foundational point that the discrimination identified in the Baldus study is structurally (and historically) embedded in Georgia's justice institutions. Yet the issue was nonetheless important because it spoke to an underlying paradox. Mandatory death penalty statutes had been declared unconstitutional in *Woodson v. North Carolina* (1976), in part because they provided "no standards to guide the jury in its inevitable exercise of the power to determine which first-degree murderers shall live and which shall die" (428 U.S. 280, 303). When a defendant was convicted of capital murder in North Carolina at the time, the obligatory corresponding sentence was execution; no lesser penalty was available for consideration. Jurors, in other words, had absolute discretion whether to sentence a defendant to death (or acquit) because they received no guidance on how and when capital punishment should be appropriately applied: for example, Jury A sentencing a black offender to death and then Jury B engaging in jury nullification to keep a white defendant off death row. Consequently, North Carolina's law left the judiciary unable to constrain the arbitrary and capricious use of sentencing power by a jury.

In *McCleskey*, O'Connor's concern was that elective death penalty laws that include statutory guidance on when executions might be imposed were also problematic because they granted jurors excessive discretionary latitude, which allowed racial prejudice to affect sentencing outcomes. Thus, when O'Connor asked whether the "Court's cases that have, since Furman, opened up to allow more discretion, were wrongly decided, and we should move back toward less discretion" (*McCleskey*, No. 84-6811, at 27:08), the keen irony was that both mandatory and optional approaches had been ineffective at preventing arbitrary and racially motivated outcomes due to juror discretion. The broader motivation behind O'Connor's inquiry was to question Boger about what statutory or procedural measures could be implemented to mend the problem of racially disproportionate death sentencing. Boger responded that Georgia had one of the most autonomous capital sentencing systems in the country and that the state "could do a better job limiting the special circumstances of capital crimes and establishing prosecutorial standards" (Poveda 2016:25). To Boger and the rest of McCleskey's legal team, the Baldus study was definitive proof of that point and the larger reality that the Supreme Court's efforts in *Gregg* to correct the problems of racially biased, arbitrary, and capricious capital sentencing had been a resounding failure.

The State of Georgia's Rebuttal

In stark contrast to Boger's impassioned defense of the Baldus study, the state of Georgia's deputy attorney general Mary Beth Westmoreland questioned the materiality of the Baldus study's statistical analysis to McCleskey's specific case. Her foremost claim was that homicide cases were improperly coded, thereby minimizing the aggravation evident in *McCleskey*. Westmoreland noted that Baldus had classified McCleskey's crime in the midrange level of aggravation but that shooting a police officer during the commission of armed robbery by an assailant with prior felony convictions fell within the highest range of aggravated crimes. She further argued that the Baldus study could not show that cases that were factually analogous to *McCleskey* did not result in a death penalty "because each case is unique on its own individual facts," albeit while conceding that there was "indication that some police officer killings did not receive a death penalty [and] some police officer killings with an armed robbery did not receive a death penalty" (*McCleskey*, No. 84-6811, at 32:42). Justice Stevens pressed Westmoreland on the matter, asking whether it was possible to state with full confidence that identical cases yielded comparable sentencing outcomes. Westmoreland deftly sidestepped the query by responding that the Baldus study failed to show that "there are similar cases in which the death penalty has not been imposed" (*id.* at 36:04).

In many ways, Westmoreland's position was brilliant in its simplicity. Understanding Boger's argument for why McCleskey was sentenced to death while other similarly situated offenders were not requires an understanding of the complex empirical rationale for how and why aggravation was coded in the Baldus study. Westmoreland, however, merely proclaimed anecdotally that killing a cop is always the highest level of aggravation in a homicide case and that statistical studies cannot definitively show whether comparable cases are indeed factually similar because they fail to account for all of the potential variables that may affect aggravation level and influence sentencing outcomes. Quite simply, she reasoned that there was too much subjectivity in prosecutorial and juror decision-making to be accurately quantified using statistical methods (see Vito and Higgins 2016). When Justices Stevens and Marshall subsequently asked Westmoreland to justify her rationale for disparaging the Baldus study's findings, she simply replied that any identified sentencing disparities could be explained by the fact that white-victim cases were systematically more serious than black-victim cases were.

> We had . . . two statisticians who . . . gave various challenges to the data base itself; the manner in which the data base was actually put together; the methodology utilized in analyzing the data base, based on the various problems with that data base; as well as going through and doing a complete analysis, based on this same data base, of all the cases, based on different sentencing outcomes, based on different aggravating circumstances, and various other factors, in an examination across the board, shows that within each of these facets, white victim cases are qualitatively different from black victim cases. They tend to have more factors such as armed robberies, rapes; more property motivated types of crimes. The black victim cases, on the other hand, based on the data presented by the petitioner, tend to arise in more circumstances involving such things as a family dispute; a barroom quarrel, if you will. And these things occurred throughout the various

sentencing stages, and throughout, as we noted ... under different aggravating circumstances, and in various categories
of cases; and is a systematic difference, which we would sub-
mit, certainly accounts for any disparity that may exist in the
sentencing process itself. (*McCleskey*, No. 84-6811, at 38:08)

As she stood before the Court, Westmoreland proclaimed
that the very nature of homicides among black Americans
in Georgia was *qualitatively different* from those involving whites. Blackness and its attendant social attributes, she
argued, were the *actual source* of the sentencing differentials
highlighted by the Baldus study. At the heart of her reasoning was the supposed fact that murders committed by and
against black Americans were invariably the product of
drunkenness, crimes of passion, or jealousy or generally were
less aggravated, which allowed the state to charge them out
at less than first-degree homicide, thereby resulting in fewer
death sentences.

To make such an argument, Westmoreland had to convince the Court that the most thorough empirical study of
capital punishment ever completed was fatally flawed to the
point of misrepresenting the cause of racial disparities in
Georgia capital sentencing. She also suggested that the state's
expert statisticians, Joseph Katz and Roger Buford, had properly identified those mistakes even though their analyses had
never been properly scrutinized via peer review but rather
by state officials who had a vested interest in their findings
contradicting those of the Baldus study. Just a short time earlier, Boger had been questioned extensively about the Baldus
study's validity; he pointed out that a significant race effect
remained constant even though the data had been recoded
several times at the request of the district court. Yet none of

the presiding justices probed Westmoreland about the statistical examinations completed by Katz and Buford, whom she vaguely remarked had given "various challenges" to Baldus's statistical database, determined it to be flawed, and concluded that black-victim cases consistently had more mitigating characteristics than white-victim cases did (*McCleskey*, No. 84-6811, at 38:08). It was a cunning argument because Westmoreland did not necessarily need to convince the Court that the Baldus study had no inherent value. She simply needed to induce skepticism that its findings could be generalized to infer discriminatory outcomes in Georgia's death sentencing practices. The statistical rebuttal offered by Katz and Buford was more than adequate to fashion the position that so many potential variables are subjectively considered by prosecutors and jurors on a case-to-case basis—particularly when considering that all capital cases are factually unique and therefore not subject to comparison—that their underlying intentions could not accurately be evaluated through statistical regression models.

There was something deeply insidious—and fundamentally ironic—about Westmoreland's disclosure that the state's own analysis indicated that white-victim cases were more aggravated and qualitatively different from consistently less severe black-victim cases. She had essentially told the Court that subjective variability inherent to prosecuting capital cases rendered statistical data an unreliable indicator of discrimination while at the same time using her own empirical evaluation to imply that blackness was a characteristic in determining criminal conduct and crime severity. The very premise of such an argument was laced with assumptions of biological determinism, which Westmoreland never explicitly expressed or appeared to endorse but also made no effort to clarify other than claiming that these facts were corroborated by the data review performed by Katz and Buford.

In positing that *black murders are different*, Westmoreland buttressed her argument on the same principles of legal bifurcation that had long ago been perverted to justify the need for Black Codes and lynching. Her presentation to the Court was sterilized almost entirely of race, focused instead on explaining how and why the sentencing disparities identified in the Baldus study were the product of criminal aggravation, which was consistently more severe in white-victim cases. With deft rhetorical sleight of hand, Westmoreland suggested that there were too many potential variables affecting sentencing outcomes to take seriously the Baldus study's finding that race plays an impermissible role in whether a homicide case in Georgia results in execution or a lesser punishment, only to then assert that the state's much-less-credible data analysis could be used to generalize consistently greater criminal aggravation in white-victim cases.

The lack of clearly identifiable purposeful discrimination was ultimately the crux of the matter for Westmoreland, notwithstanding that "the correlation that the Baldus study shows between race and death sentencing in Georgia is two-and-a-half times greater than the proven correlation between cigarette smoking and heart disease" (David Bruck, quoted in Lewis 1987:A31). Her contention that the Baldus study failed to illustrate any racist intent on the part of specific actors during McCleskey's trial established a nearly impossible burden of proof for petitioners claiming equal protection violations in capital cases (someone must effectively proclaim oneself publicly to be bigoted). She further reframed sentencing disproportionalities as the product of prosecutors implementing procedure based on the unique characteristics of each given case and not resulting from institutional problems embedded in a flawed system. Accordingly, Westmoreland concluded that McCleskey's trial was evidence that Georgia's death penalty system operated as the Court intended in *Gregg*. In doing so, she cleverly prompted the Court's moderate and conservative justices to focus on individual decision-making in lieu of systemic bias as the constitutional threshold for establishing discriminatory intent in capital sentencing.

4

All Discrimination Is Not Considered Equal

When Jack Boger walked out of the Supreme Court following oral arguments in *McCleskey v. Kemp*, he should have been reasonably confident about his chances of prevailing. After all, he was armed with compelling empirical data suggesting that Georgia's death process was replete with systemic racial bias. Mary Beth Westmoreland, on the other hand, had relied on speculative and highly inflammatory racialized characterizations of homicide offending and victimization among black Americans. Boger also knew he had secured the votes of the Court's liberal justices William Brennan and Thurgood Marshall, given their consistent legal opposition to capital punishment; and it remained possible that the Baldus study would win over more moderate and conservative justices such as John Paul Stevens, Lewis Powell, and perhaps even Sandra Day O'Connor. Justice Brennan, in particular, loomed as an important figure over the Court. For decades alongside Marshall, he had shepherded Warren Court majorities as "the behind-the-scenes architect for many of the landmark rulings of the Court's liberal era—in desegregation, school prayer, the rights of crime suspects, the freedom of the press, women's rights, and the right to abortion" (Savage 1992:10). Included among Brennan's successes was a blistering indictment of capital punishment in *Furman v. Georgia* (and its companion cases, *Jackson v. Georgia* and *Branch v. Texas*), when in 1972 the High Court declared the nation's death penalty unconstitutional by a deeply divisive

5–4 vote. It was in *Furman* that Brennan shaped his personal jurisprudence on capital punishment (see Tabak 1991), arguing in part that when so few murderers are sent to death row and executed, "the conclusion is virtually inescapable that [capital punishment] is being inflicted arbitrarily. Indeed, it smacks of little more than a lottery system" (*Furman*, 408 U.S. at 293). Although the death penalty was reinstated four years later in *Gregg v. Georgia*, Brennan and Marshall never wavered in their opposition to capital punishment and the disparate harm it inflicted across racial and socioeconomic demographic lines.

By the time Warren Burger retired from the Court in 1986, conservative opposition to Brennan and his furtherance of legal egalitarianism advanced by the Warren Court had sparked deep ideological divisions among the sitting justices. This prompted the Reagan administration to seek a new chief justice with the conservative ethos needed to curtail the "judicial coup d'etat" of activist liberal justices such as Brennan who had "established the Court as a 'superlegislature,' overturning with no constitutional authority the judgments of elected representatives" (Lazarus 1998:8). Reagan's choice was William Rehnquist, a staunch conservative who had served as associate justice since 1971. Rehnquist was born and raised to working-class parents near Milwaukee, Wisconsin, and his distinguished legal career began as a law clerk for Associate Justice Robert H. Jackson in 1952. It was during that year that Rehnquist authored a memorandum opposing federally enforced school desegregation in which he defended the Jim Crow "separate but equal" doctrine. "I realize that it is an unpopular and unhumanitarian position, for which I have been excoriated by 'liberal' colleagues," Rehnquist wrote, "but I think *Plessy v. Ferguson* was right and should be re-affirmed" (1952:325).[1]

Although Rehnquist later attempted to distance himself from *Plessy* by suggesting that the support of segregation actually reflected the views of Justice Jackson, there were other alleged incidents that painted a troubling picture. There were rumors that during the 1960s, he had served as a poll watcher in Phoenix, sometimes harassing black and Hispanic voters while actively opposing voter-registration initiatives and a local antidiscrimination ordinance. Again, he denied the allegations; but uncertainty about whether "issues of racial justice and nondiscrimination were not a high priority" to Rehnquist raised concerns (whether fairly or not) and suggested insensitivity to the plights of petitioners such as Warren McCleskey (see Liptak 2005). His legacy indeed reveals profound antipathy toward death penalty inmates, of whom Rehnquist lamented, "it is too bad that drawing and quartering has been abolished," because he believed they routinely employed legal obstructionism to avoid their executions. Edward Lazarus further remarks that Rehnquist "thought the forces of abolition were demeaning the rule of law and that it was high time for the Court to usher other 'fitting candidates' to their appointed fate" (1998:140).

In many ways, the roots of Rehnquist's staunch support of capital punishment reflected why he was considered the justice who most prominently embodied the judicial philosophy of the Reagan administration (Savage 1992), which included curbing federal authority in civil rights enforcement, diminishing oversight of school desegregation, undoing efforts to eliminate de jure discrimination in higher education, restricting affirmative action, and dismantling workers' rights in employment discrimination cases (see Davis and Graham 1995).[2] As far back as 1952, Rehnquist had already established his opposition to federal habeas corpus and commitment to protecting states' rights (Lazarus 1998). When considered in relation to his alleged support of segregation and voter-suppression efforts, the underlying sentiments were not too far removed from the "southern strategy" adopted to preserve the old Confederacy from federal intrusion following the successes of the civil rights movement by appealing to the racist inclinations of poor and working-class white voters. By the time Ronald Reagan ascended to the presidency, southern resistance to the stubborn legacy of intolerance had evolved into promotion of states'-rights narratives using coded racial rhetoric that demonized blacks as lazy, irresponsible, and accustomed to a culture of poverty and criminality. Whereas whites were framed as industrious and law-abiding citizens, public officials and media imagery surreptitiously cast blacks as taking advantage of the system by abusing social services and obtaining jobs undeservedly due to affirmative action (see M. Alexander 2010). For decades, Reagan told voters about a six-figure-income-earning "welfare queen" who "has 80 names, 30 addresses, 12 Social Security Cards, is collecting veterans' benefits on 4 non-existing deceased husband, . . . [is] collecting Medicaid, is getting food stamps, and she is collecting welfare under each of her names." In a similar anecdote, Reagan spoke about a "slum dweller" living luxuriously in government-subsidized housing projects funded by taxpayer dollars (*New York Times* 1976:51).

Of course, Reagan knew that these stories were largely fabrications, and he was careful to never directly locate housing projects in minority neighborhoods or identify the welfare queen as a black woman.[3] He instead sought to articulate and fortify divisions between those whom he implied would cheat the system and the white voters to whom he was speaking. Donald R. Culverson contends, "The speeches emphasized how 'they,' the abusers, enjoyed lives of leisure, whereas 'we' worked harder than ever before, with little chance of getting ahead. The welfare-queen story played well with small-town and suburban audiences, and its reference to 'a woman in Chicago' left little doubt about the implied racial identity of the abuser. The story acquired a life of its own [and] resonated with the experiences and interpretations of blocs of disenchanted white voters" (2007:129–130). Using racially sanitized rhetoric, Reagan furtively categorized people of color (and the poor) as bearing personal responsibility for their social and personal failings and thus as undeserving of a social safety net funded by the taxes of hardworking Americans. Outwardly, Reagan framed his message as one of limited government, and it contrasted favorably against more liberal Democratic assertions that social conditions were the primary cause of crime, which needed to be combated with an ever-expanding array of antipoverty and civil rights programs (see M. Alexander 2010). In truth, Reagan purposefully sought to polarize voters along racial lines by exploiting white animus toward blacks and cultivating disdain for the economically poor. None of this had emerged out of the blue; it was inspired by a unique brand of explicitly racist southern identity politics but instead implemented "the use of a race-free political language [that] proved critical to building a broad-based" domestic coalition (Edsall and Edsall 1991:138). This was the intended message when Reagan promoted states' rights and characterized the 1965 Voting Rights Act as "humiliating to the South" (Krugman 2007). He was speaking not only to the disaffection that many white voters harbored for people of color but also to the segregationist history and inclination of southerners to fear how the federal government had stripped away their culture and way of life by enacting policies to advance the undeserving at their expense.

Seeking the Swing Vote

Only once in Jack Boger's opening remarks in *McCleskey v. Kemp* was any reference made to what is an institutionalized culture of white resistance based on antifederal sentiment, states' rights, and racial oppression. He used most of his allotted time to try and inform the Court of the Baldus study's core findings and the difficulty in reversing Georgia's history of inequality. Boger certainly understood that "the factual complexity of the data and related evidence ensured that [he] could not walk through vast numbers of complementary statistical findings [related to the Baldus study] in such a short period. . . . In consequence, the key seemed to be a quick and accurate assessment of the key themes—the historical racial bias in Georgia sentencing, the thoroughness of Baldus's research, the multiplicity of his analytical method—that race was indeed playing a real and significant role" (Boger 2016). He also might have rightly expected the majority of the Court's sitting justices to recognize the historical and empirical correlation between race and capital sentencing in Georgia. After all, a judicial arbiter need not be African American or directly affected by systemic discrimination to grasp its existence in social and legal institutions, particularly when it had been so undeniably exposed by the Baldus study. At the very least, he was well aware that the two most influential liberal justices, William Brennan and Thurgood Marshall, had drawn a line in the sand on capital punishment; he also expected John Paul Stevens and Harry Blackmun to join them in ruling Georgia's death penalty unconstitutional (see Dorin 1994).

Needing only one more vote to carry the day, Boger had to turn one of the remaining justices to his side. Aside from Rehnquist, Byron White was perhaps least likely to vote for McCleskey. Although White had asserted in *Gregg* that Georgia's capital statute should be struck down if data were to show that sentencing was arbitrary and capricious, his expressed jurisprudence in subsequent capital cases was undeniably pro–death penalty. Some observers believed Boger could sway Scalia following his critical response to Westmoreland's assertion that white-victim cases are qualitatively different from black-victim cases, when he implied that the Baldus study analyzes a sufficient number and variety of variables to debunk that argument (*McCleskey*, No. 84-6811, at 39:28). In retrospect, however, Scalia's vote was never in play, on the basis of the substance of his *McCleskey* memorandum, in which he suggests that the case taken to its logical conclusion would throw the entire justice system into chaos and facilitate additional cases in other states where data would similarly show inferences of discrimination. Furthermore, Scalia indicated that "no showing of racial discrimination in the death sentencing process—no matter how strong or direct—would violate the Eighth or Fourteenth Amendments" because he found "its presence to be of no legal consequence" (S. Johnson 2002:127–128).

Sandra Day O'Connor was another possibility. Boger perceived her "as honestly grappling with the conceptual peculiarities" of the case, including "the principal remedial question [of] whether the Court should somehow require more death sentences in the future, or fewer (To wit, is the problem too many death sentences, or alternatively, too few?)" (Boger 2016). At the time, however, O'Connor was closely aligned politically with Rehnquist, Scalia, and White, so it is unclear whether she ever really entertained the possibility of voting for McCleskey. Years later, she publicly expressed concern about capital sentencing fairness and wrongful executions, noting in an interview, "if statistics are

any indication, the system may well be allowing some innocent defendants to be executed" (Associated Press 2001). That
left Lewis Powell as Boger's most likely swing vote, and Powell was not without reason for voting in McCleskey's favor.
Powell had previously found a prima facie case in *Batson v.
Kentucky* (1986) solely on the basis of a prosecutor's procliv-
ity to use peremptory challenges to remove prospective black
American jurors in a black defendant's case (see Dorin 1984).
He also heard arguments in a number of death penalty cases,
including *Furman v. Georgia*, in which he established that
equal protection claims apply to black defendants if they can
show that their sentences are disproportionately harsher than
those of other defendants charged with the same offense, although he also suggested that evolving standards of criminal
justice have reduced the risk of racial bias in capital cases.

Moreover, Powell had voted with the majority in *Bazemore v. Friday* (1986), which reversed a lower court ruling
that statistical regression analyses typically used to establish patterns of causation—that is, changes in a dependent
variable (e.g., capital sentencing) are produced through its
association with independent variables, such as race, social
class, and gender—were insufficient proof of disparate treatment because they failed to account for all potential mea-
surable variables that might account for wage disparities
between black and white employees. Specifically, the Court
noted, "A regression analysis that includes less than 'all mea-
surable variables' may serve to prove a plaintiff's case [be-
cause] a plaintiff in a Title VII [employment discrimination]
suit need not prove discrimination with scientific certainty;
rather, his or her burden is to prove discrimination by a preponderance of the evidence. . . . As long as the court may
fairly conclude, in light of all the evidence, that it is more
likely than not that impermissible discrimination exists, the

plaintiff is entitled to prevail" (*Bazemore v. Friday*, 478 U.S. 385, 400–401 (1986)). The Court's ruling in *Bazemore* is significant because it established that statistical evidence could be proof of discrimination even when failing to account for all of the principal variables producing unequal outcomes.[4] When considered in combination with Powell's earlier majority opinion in *McDonnell Douglas Corp. v. Green* (1973), which articulated the burden of proof to establish disparate treatment under Title VII of the 1964 Civil Rights Act as including direct evidence (someone acts overtly racist) *and* circumstantial evidence that establishes an inference of discrimination (see T. Green 1999), it was reasonable for Boger to believe that Powell might be sympathetic to his argument in *McCleskey v. Kemp*.

In reality, though, any hope that Boger might have had for attaining five votes was entirely unfounded. Although he plainly recognized Byron White's hostility during oral arguments (Boger 2016), Boger did not know at the time that White had already taken "the extremely unusual (and perhaps unprecedented) step of sending Justices Rehnquist, Powell, O'Connor, and Scalia a detailed memo . . . urging a unified vote to reject McCleskey's claims" (Lazarus 1998:202). White's uninhibited partisanship in authoring the backroom memorandum probably helped confirm votes against McCleskey, particularly with O'Connor, who appeared conflicted during oral arguments, and Lewis Powell, who was known for reserving judgments until his peers weighed in and he rethought his own interpretations (Jeffries 1994).

Byron White's behind-the-scenes efforts reflect just how deeply divided the Supreme Court was during the 1980s. These political schisms were exacerbated when Reagan nominated William Rehnquist as chief justice with the hope that he would stunt the long-standing liberal authority of William Brennan and steer the Supreme Court sharply to the right. The result-ing internal and ideological divisions within the Court became so corrosive that they call into question the Court's integrity and the political motives of individual justices (Lazarus 1998).[5] Robert H. Stroup argues that McCleskey's chances were fur-ther harmed by his case being "litigated in a social, political, and legal context that featured a federal retrenchment from the promise to undo the continuing taint of racial discrimina-tion in U.S. society [and] before a federal judiciary increasingly reluctant to require social change through judicial decision-making" (2008:94–95). By April 1987, the Rehnquist Court had already begun reversing liberal precedents established by the Warren Court. Foremost were efforts to restrict federal habeas petitions by establishing "a series of trapdoors where any procedural wrong step, no matter how trivial, resulted in a petitioner forfeiting his claim [and] by telling states . . . that they need not provide petitioners with lawyers during [the ap-pellate] process" (Lazarus 1998:503–504).[6] For Warren McCles-key and similarly situated petitioners, the Rehnquist Court's adherence to habeas reform and commitment to protecting states' rights ultimately revealed an unwillingness to enact even nominally intrusive federal mandates to ensure that state-level judicial systems provide equal protection under the law on the basis of race (see Stroup 2008).

A Court Divided

When the Supreme Court upheld Warren McCleskey's death sentence by a 5–4 vote on April 22, 1987, the majority affirmed that a racially disproportionate capital system is not unconstitutional. Justice Lewis Powell (joined by Rehnquist, O'Connor, Scalia, and White) was tasked with authoring the majority opinion, in which he argued that aggregated statistical data of racial disparities were insufficient to sub-stantiate Eighth and Fourteenth Amendment claims of arbitrariness and discrimination in Georgia's capital sentenc-ing (see Poveda 2016).[7] Central to Powell's opinion was the assertion that petitioners such as McCleskey are obligated to show that specific individuals—including prosecutors, expert witnesses, judges, and jurors—were *purposefully* prejudiced: "McCleskey must prove that the decisionmak-ers in *his* case acted with discriminatory purpose. He offers no evidence specific to his own case that would support an inference that racial considerations played a part in his sen-tence" (*McCleskey*, 481 U.S. at 292–293, emphasis in original). Powell reached this conclusion by arguing that the Baldus study (and statistical data, more generally) merely demon-strated "a discrepancy that appears to correlate with race" while failing to definitively show that capital sentencing in Georgia was unconstitutional under the Eighth and Four-teenth Amendments (*id.* at 291–292, 306–308, 312). Although Powell conceded that the Court had accepted inferential statistical evidence in other instances, including employ-ment discrimination cases (*id.* at 293–297), he rejected its application to criminal cases where juror discretion plays a fundamental role in conviction and sentencing (Simon 1995). Accordingly, he ruled that empirical evidence of statewide sentencing disparities does not prove there exists a consti-tutionally significant risk of racial bias, noting instead that "apparent disparities in sentencing are an inevitable part of our criminal justice system" (*id.* at 312).

This point is particularly salient because it indicates that Powell and the concurring justices acknowledged that some racial prejudice in death penalty cases is acceptable. At the very least, they refused the position that even the slightest trace of bias in a capital trial—or any criminal proceeding, more generally—is sufficient to produce a constitutional violation. They therefore reasoned that McCleskey's Eighth Amendment rights were not violated because widespread sentencing disparities that correlate with race do not necessarily signify a significant risk of racial discrimination in Georgia's capital sentencing for any particular defendant and in any given case. Notwithstanding that Jack Boger had "developed some historical background to Georgia's justice system, going back to slavery and Georgia's dual system of criminal law that differentiated between punishments for black and whites" (Poveda 2016:27), Powell discarded these concerns as too distant in the past and therefore functionally irrelevant to McCleskey's specific case. In doing so, he placed tremendous (and perhaps blind) faith in the belief that neither biased jurors nor court personnel nor institutionalized discrimination in the Georgia justice system significantly contributed to the sentencing disparities identified in the Baldus study.

Justice Powell's majority opinion also rejected the common parlance of "disparate impact" established in employment and housing discrimination cases, which assumes that policies and practices are discriminatory if they adversely affect protected classes in a disproportionate manner even if they are intended to function impartially. In *Village of Arlington Heights v. Metropolitan Housing Development Corp.* (1977), Powell previously argued that "sometimes a clear pattern, unexplainable on grounds other than race, emerges from the effect of the state action even when the governing legislation appears neutral on its face" and that absent an overtly discriminatory outcome, "the Court must look to other evidence" because "impact alone is not determinative" (429 U.S. 252, 266). With regard to instances of housing discrimination, Powell's opinion in *Arlington* seems to suggest that when evidence of disparate impact gives rise to an inference of discrimination, then discrimination itself is evident. Yet this criterion was not considered in *McCleskey v. Kemp* because the Court applied the disparate treatment standard, requiring the petitioner to supply direct evidence that his particular case was uniquely harmed by intentional acts of purposeful racism.

Had the Court applied the disparate impact standard, it is difficult to imagine that the majority could have held that the racialized sentencing discrepancies identified by the Baldus study were "a far cry from the major systemic defects identified in *Furman* (*McCleskey*, 481 U.S. at 313). Instead, the majority essentially held that claims of discrimination require a higher standard of proof for the death penalty, when a petitioner's life is at stake, than in fair-housing cases. Although Boger had argued that the Baldus study proved that the state of Georgia acted with discriminatory purpose, the majority rejected this contention outright. Powell made clear that the Court would not infer discriminatory intent and stressed that there was no evidence to suggest that "the Georgia legislature enacted or maintained the death penalty statute *because of* an anticipated racially discriminatory effect" (*id.* at 298, emphasis in original). For Powell, the matter at hand was not so much whether racial prejudice interfered in some form with Georgia's capital sentencing procedure, because he acknowledged that possibility existed. The substantive question he and the concurring justices posed in *McCleskey* "is at what point that risk becomes constitutionally unacceptable" (*id.* at 309).

The Dissenting Bloc

There is a particularly ominous passage in Justice Brennan's *McCleskey* dissent where he paints a narrative portrait of Warren McCleskey consulting his attorney about whether he would be sentenced to death. Counsel would be forced to reply that nothing about his personal or criminal background nor the facts of his case would be more important in determining McCleskey's fate than the color of his skin and the fact that his victim was white. "The story could be told in a variety of ways," Brennan wrote, "but McCleskey could not fail to grasp its essential narrative line: there was a significant chance that race would play a prominent role in determining if he lived or died" (*McCleskey*, 481 U.S. at 321). Although the dissenting justices were not in complete alignment—Justices Blackmun and Stevens only concurred in part with the absolute rebuke of capital punishment proffered by Justices Brennan and Marshall—they all agreed that Georgia's legacy of racial discrimination persevered in contemporary criminal justice practices and contributed to systemic problems of arbitrary and discriminatory death penalty sentencing in Georgia. Justice Brennan forcefully refuted any possibility that the Baldus study's statistical analysis might be flawed, describing the harsher treatment of black assailants of white victims as an "intractable reality of the death penalty" (*id.* at 320). It was noted that blacks convicted of killing whites were sentenced to death at 22 times the rate of blacks who killed blacks; and prosecutors sought capital punishment in 70 percent of cases with black offenders and white victims, as opposed to only 19 percent of the time with a white defendant and black victim (see Vito and Higgins 2016). Based on these data, Brennan concluded that the safeguards built into the Georgia statute by *Gregg* had failed to remedy the problems of capricious, arbitrary, and discriminatory capital sentencing.

Brennan did not necessarily believe that Georgia's history of institutional prejudice and discriminatory social practices, characterized so prominently by Jim Crow segregation and persistent efforts to resist federal integration and civil rights initiatives, justified "automatic condemnation of current" capital practices (*McCleskey*, 481 U.S. at 332). He instead insisted that any pragmatic observer would have to consider the historical totality of Georgia's cultural, political, and criminal justice practices when assessing the merits of the statistical data presented in *McCleskey*. Given these realities, it was Brennan's contention that the evidence of disparate treatment merely had to indicate that there was substantial risk that the punishment would be inflicted in an arbitrary and capricious manner (see *Furman*). Bearing in mind the Baldus analysis, Brennan viewed the possibility of constitutional violations and miscarriage due to the irrational influence of racial prejudice, whether purposeful or by unintended consequence, as "intolerable by any imaginable standard" (*McCleskey*, 481 U.S. at 325). As a matter of consensus, the dissenting justices agreed that permitting the state of Georgia, by design or default, to segregate justice, as the Baldus study seemed to reveal, was tantamount to turning back the judicial clock—at least symbolically—to the Jim Crow mandates of *Plessy v. Ferguson*.[8] From a constitutional perspective, the very contention was disconcerting, considering that the Supreme Court had emphatically established in landmark cases such as *Hirabayashi v. United States* (1943), *Brown v. Board of Education of Topeka* (1954), and *Loving v. Virginia* (1967) that race functioned as an unconditional means of discrimination. Justice Marshall's voice on this point is especially salient, as he decried the majority for "shrinking from the implications of McCleskey's evidence" and endorsing the "categorical assessment of the worth of human beings according to color" (*McCleskey*, 481 U.S. at 335–336).

Greasing the Wheels and Hastening Death

By setting aside the Baldus study and its recognition of ongoing racialized capital sentencing practices in Georgia, the Supreme Court seemingly ignored its "own recognition of the persistent danger that racial attitudes may affect criminal proceedings" (*McCleskey*, 481 U.S. at 329). Alongside numerous failures to enact federal racial-justice legislation between 1988 and 1994, which would have allowed for consideration of statistical data as evidence of discrimination during the appellate phase of death penalty cases, the years following *McCleskey* were a windfall for prosecutors and other public officials. With violent-crime rates at record highs during the late 1980s and early 1990s, there was considerable public support for capital punishment, peaking at 80 percent favorability in 1994 (Gallup 2017). Legislators across the political spectrum championed executions in order to appear tough on crime. During the 1992 presidential election, for example, Bill Clinton responded to the surge in the polls of his Democratic primary opponent, Michael Dukakis, by vocalizing strong support for the death penalty and allowing the execution of Ricky Ray Rector to proceed despite compelling evidence of profound mental incapacitation. Following Rector's arrest for the shooting death of Arthur Criswell at an Arkansas restaurant, Rector later shot and killed the police officer taking him into custody and then himself in a failed suicide attempt that inflicted such severe trauma that it "resulted in the severance of about three inches of the left frontal pole, . . . commonly referred to in medical terms as a frontal lobotomy" (*Rector v. Clark*, 923 F.2d 570, 571 n.2 (8th Cir. 1991)). Rector was left with considerable brain damage and unable to comprehend the magnitude of his death sentence, at one point asking prison staff to save the slice of pecan pie from his last meal *for later* so he could eat it after the execution (see Frady 1993).

Critics condemned Clinton for exploiting Rector's race and mental state in the name of political opportunism by seeking to showcase a strong approach to criminal justice while diverting attention away from budding scandal over his extramarital affair with Gennifer Flowers (Frady 1993; Hitchens 1999). The political traction to be gained by endorsing executions and other tough-on-crime policies often leads politicians such as Clinton to promote their support for even the most controversial executions or simply to advocate for stern penal sanctions that do not "coddle" criminals. Considering that the Supreme Court had already rejected the Baldus study and that it was unlikely another case would emerge with more compelling evidence, by the late 1980s there was little concern that the federal judiciary would suddenly abolish the death penalty. While trial courts and prosecutors were still subject to judicial review, the Supreme Court's ruling in *McCleskey v. Kemp* left them virtually invulnerable to critical social science and the risk that statistical inference could reveal any bias or prejudice existing in criminal justice proceedings.

By this time, the Rehnquist Court had also taken steps to severely restrict habeas petitions, meaning petitioners' claims were far less likely to be heard, let alone receive favorable rulings from appellate proceedings. During a 1990 speech at the American Law Institute, William Rehnquist went so far as to publicly request that Congress pass a law limiting capital petitioners to no more than one habeas appeal, arguing that the length of time between an offender receiving the death penalty and the sentence actually being carried out reflected a "serious malfunction in our legal system" (Greenhouse 1990:A1). Rehnquist himself had never personally voted to overturn an execution from the time he was first appointed to the Court until his elevation to chief justice. Likewise, the Court over which he presided regularly upheld death sentences in even the most controversial of cases between 1986 to 2002, rejecting challenges to the constitutionality of executing juvenile and mentally incapacitated offenders and refusing to overturn any death sentence on the basis of ineffective counsel (Chemerinsky 2006). In *Herrera v. Collins* (1993), the Court even ruled that it is not necessarily unconstitutional to execute an innocent person, since "claims of actual innocence based on newly discovered evidence have never been held to state a ground for federal habeas relief absent an independent constitutional claim" (506 U.S. at 400), and errors of fact "discovered too late in the day to file a new trial motion" should be remedied by executive clemency (*id.* at 417). But it was the Court's drastic limiting of habeas relief that really accelerated the number of executions performed throughout the 1990s, and Warren McCleskey was again a central figure in that legal fight.

In chapter 2, the facts surrounding Offie Evans's jailhouse testimony were discussed, along with allegations that state officials concealed a plea deal they had made with Evans. Those actions had, in fact, constituted a *Massiah* violation, which occurs when government officials elicit statements from defendants about themselves after the point when the state's decision to prosecute formally attaches the Sixth Amendment right to counsel (*Massiah v. United States*, 377 U.S. 201 (1964)). At the time of McCleskey's original trial, Evans's confession claim helped secure McCleskey's conviction and eventual death sentence. However, Jack Boger later described Evans as "a man on a mission" who was working as a police informant when he secured the alleged confession, which occurred subsequent to the conference of McCleskey's right to counsel (*McCleskey v. Zant*, No. 89-7024 [oral arguments Oct. 30, 1990], at 5:58). Despite the concerns of Boger and his legal team, they neglected to include the *Massiah* violation in McCleskey's original habeas petition. Boger and Robert Stroup were both certain that a Sixth Amendment violation had occurred but lacked evidence of impropriety because both the state of Georgia and Evans denied a deal was made in exchange for his testimony. During oral arguments in *McCleskey v. Zant*, Boger depicted conspiratorial misconduct by state police officers, prosecutors, and other state officials in denying McCleskey's lawyers evidence and failing to inform jurors that Evans had received special treatment in exchange for his testimony. Boger noted that the collusion between Evans, law enforcement, and the trial prosecutor, Russell Parker, had devastating consequences during the original criminal trial because "it really sounded like McCleskey himself had volunteered most of this information" (*id.* at 7:02).

When the state finally turned over documentation proving Evans had received a deal that was disclosed neither to defense counsel nor to jurors (itself a *Brady* violation),[9] McCleskey's counsel swiftly filed a second habeas petition based on this newly discovered evidence. When that case—*McCleskey v. Zant*—reached the Supreme Court in 1990, Boger told the Court that Evans's written statement had been on file with the state for years but never turned over to him, which is why the *Massiah* violation could not be included on the first habeas petition (see Simon 1995). As in *McCleskey v. Kemp*, the state of Georgia was represented by Mary Beth Westmoreland, who rebutted Boger's claim by arguing that no efforts were made to conceal Evans's written statement and that defense counsel simply lacked "reasonable diligence" in failing to request all the available evidence (*Zant*, No. 89-7024, at 45:26). Justice Brennan questioned how it was possible that the only piece of evidence not turned over to the defense was the Evans statement, asking, "when a defense lawyer is trying to get access to all statements and pertinent records, how does it just so happen there is one very important document somehow gets lost?" (*id.* at 34:44). Westmoreland challenged that the state had no constitutional obligation to provide defense counsel with the Evans statement prior to the criminal trial and that nothing was done to prevent McCleskey's lawyers from obtaining it after the trial was over. At one point, Thurgood Marshall asked Westmoreland whether she was "trying to convince" the Court "that defense counsel was aware of the existence of this statement." Westmoreland responded, "he should have been" since "defense counsel certainly was told there was a statement" (*id.* at 28:22). This led Marshall to ask whether a mistake had been made, to which Westmoreland responded, "yes, Your Honor, that is absolutely correct" (*id.* at 31:52). When Marshall pressed further, questioning whether McCleskey should die because of an error made by his lawyers, Westmoreland replied in the affirmative: "Your Honor, my position is that counsel made a mistake, that that constitutes an abuse of the writ, and that there is no miscarriage of justice in this case because there is no question of Mr. McCleskey's guilt in this matter. Yes, Your Honor, that is our position in this matter" (*id.* at 32:04). The Court concurred with Westmoreland by a 6–3 majority, ruling that petitioners should include all relevant claims in their initial petition. Successive habeas requests would therefore not be allowed in most cases, and federal courts could refuse to review any subsequent appeal regardless of whether petitioners intended to exploit the system or any abuse of writ had occurred (see Kirchmeier 2015).

In *Zant*, the Supreme Court agreed with the earlier circuit court ruling that the lack of Offie Evans's signed written statement should not have prevented the *Massiah* claim from being raised in the initial habeas petition.[10] Justice Kennedy in his majority opinion explained that the defense was aware "based on testimony and questioning at trial . . . that [McCleskey] had confessed the murder during jail-cell conversations with Evans, knew that Evans claimed to be a relative of Ben Wright during the conversations, and knew that Evans told the police about the conversations" (*Zant*, 499 U.S. at 498–499). The Court therefore determined that McCleskey's counsel should have known about and provided proof of the *Massiah* violation at the time of the first habeas petition, notwithstanding that Boger and Stroup did not yet have any idea Evans was acting as a police informant. The problem, however, was that in order to prove that the *Massiah* violation had occurred, McCleskey's attorneys first needed to show that the state had committed a *Brady* violation by failing to provide the defense access to Evans's signed written statement, the evidence of which was not discovered until after that first habeas petition had already been rejected. Kennedy's reasoning was at least partly based on his acceptance of Westmoreland's argument that no *Brady* violation had occurred since McCleskey's trial lawyer, John Turner, was to blame for failing to acquire the statement document. But the fact remained that when Offie Evans attested to McCleskey's supposed confession, neither he nor the prosecution had disclosed to jurors that Evans received a deal in exchange for his testimony.

The ruling was devastating for petitioners such as McCleskey because the Court established a far more restrictive legal standard for both obtaining relief and filing successive habeas petitions in a single death penalty case. Justice Kennedy explained that these habeas limitations were necessary to reduce the overall duration of litigation so courts could more efficiently achieve finality in capital cases (*Zant*, 499 U.S. at

491–493). But whereas petitioners previously had broad lee-way to file additional habeas claims so long as their efforts did not constitute abuse of writ, state and federal courts after *Zant* had little reason even to review, let alone to overturn, death sentences. In California, for example, the state su-preme court went from affirming 8 percent of death cases it reviewed from 1978 through 1986 to an astounding 94 per-cent between 1986 and 1996 (Uelmen 2009). Alongside the courts showing little interest in decelerating the death ma-chine, politicians and judges sympathetic to capital punish-ment were swept into office; and many incumbents endorsed executions as a means of catering to public opinion and po-sitioning themselves as anticrime advocates. The staggering rise in death sentences affirmed by the Supreme Court of California was a direct result of three justices being removed during a 1986 election, "largely on the campaign claim that votes against these three would be three votes in favor of the death penalty" (Uelmen 2009:498). State legislators similarly augmented the availability and use of capital punishment statutes, which in many cases led to the authorization of new aggravating factors that broadened the scope of homicides eligible for death penalty consideration.

On the federal level, Congress was unable to pass a Racial Justice Act in 1988 but that same year did enact legislation to reinstate federal executions for the first time since being struck down by *Furman* in 1972. Ratification of the Anti-Drug Abuse Act of 1988 authorized capital punishment for anyone convicted of homicide committed as part of an ongo-ing criminal enterprise, such as a drug cartel. Several years later, the federal death penalty was expanded with the bipar-tisan passage of the omnibus Violent Crime Control and Law Enforcement Act of 1994; it contained a variety of provisos that strengthened penal sanctions and fostered dramatic growth in the prison system, including the delineation of new federal crimes, an assault weapons ban, funding to combat violence against women, the elimination of higher education for prison inmates, introduction of sex-offender registries, and the creation of 60 new offenses eligible for federal capital punishment. Then, in 1996, President Clinton signed into law the Antiterrorism and Effective Death Penalty Act (AEDPA), which ended up gutting habeas corpus and the authority of federal judges to review and provide relief in capital cases. Recall that the Supreme Court had already taken measures to limit habeas review, such as placing severe restrictions on petitioners' ability to file successive petitions, in *Zant*. The AEDPA fortified those measures and attempted to speed up the appellate process by virtually ensuring that petitioners received no more than one habeas claim, which needed to be filed within a strictly regulated time frame. Specifically, the AEDPA stipulated that federal courts may only intervene and review habeas claims when state court proceedings "resulted in a decision that was contrary to, or involved an unreasonable application of, clearly established Federal law" or were "based on an unreasonable determination of the facts in light of the evidence presented" (Pub. L. 104-132, 110 Stat. 1219).

Initially, this meant that federal courts were required to let stand all state court rulings unless it was shown that the law was applied improperly or in error, thereby resulting in the petitioner's unlawful imprisonment (Reinhardt 2015). However, in *Williams v. Terry* (2000), the Supreme Court ruled that petitioners should not be granted habeas relief even when state courts reach incorrect decisions due to a misinterpretation of Supreme Court precedent. Simply put, state court verdicts reached in error did not necessarily violate federal law. Death-row inmates were left trapped in a "twisted labyrinth of deliberately crafted legal obstacles that make it as difficult for habeas petitioners to succeed in pursuing the Writ as it would be for a Supreme Court Justice to strike out Babe Ruth, Joe DiMaggio, and Mickey Mantle in succession—even with the Chief Justice calling balls and strikes" (Reinhardt 2015:1220). Meanwhile, federal judges often found themselves unable to properly address habeas claims and therefore helpless to protect petitioners from procedural gaffes that were likely to cause—if they had not already caused—unlawful convictions, unjust sentencing decisions, and wrongful executions.[11]

All of that hardly seemed to matter. With widespread public support for capital punishment and little judicial or legislative resistance to swelling execution rates, the tolerance of racial sentencing inequities in *McCleskey v. Kemp* and the erosion of habeas protections through ensuing Supreme Court rulings and the AEDPA allowed the death penalty to become an almost unstoppable force during the 1990s.

5

Reaffirming "Separate but Equal"

By the turn of the 21st century, the number of executions performed yearly in the United States had reached its highest level since the early 1950s. With public support for the death penalty hovering around 70 percent (Gallup 2017), few people at the time would have predicted that the country was on the brink of a precipitous decline in the use of capital punishment. But the shift was already well under way (see figure 5.1). In 2001, there were 155 death sentences imposed nationally, down from 315 in 1996; it also marked the first time since 1980 that fewer than 200 death sentences were levied in a single year (Death Penalty Information Center 2017a). This drop resulted from the convergence of forces that helped pique social concerns about the efficacy and fairness of state-sanctioned executions. First, several important research investigations not only reaffirmed the Baldus study's finding that race pervasively affects capital sentencing decisions but also identified a staggering amount of trial error resulting from bias, incompetence, and professional misconduct. Two studies published by Columbia University researchers examined 4,578 capital cases; they concluded that nearly 70 percent of all death sentences reviewed by appellate courts between 1973 and 1995 were "seriously flawed" and contained errors so grievous that they "undermined the reliability of the outcome or otherwise 'harmed' the defendant" (Liebman, Fagan, and West 2000:4). They also identified the most common forms of error as incompetent defense lawyers who fail

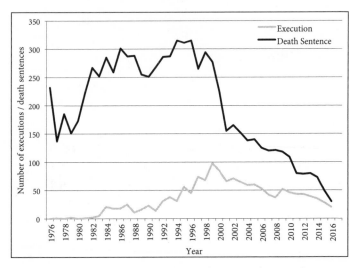

Figure 5.1. Death sentences and executions by year in the United States, 1976–2016. Source: Death Penalty Information Center 2017a, 2017b.

to identify or present evidence that their clients are either innocent or undeserving of the death penalty, police and prosecutors who knowingly suppress exculpatory evidence, jurors who are misinformed about the law, and judges or jurors who are biased (Liebman, Fagan, and West 2000; Liebman et al. 2002). It was concluded that 73 percent of cases retried on appeal resulted in the defendant being sentenced to less than death, *with 9 percent resulting in acquittals* (Liebman et al. 2002).

The Columbia studies were profound in their implications. If serious mistakes (or misconduct) were discerned in the vast majority of capital cases and took multiple judicial reviews to identify, it was highly unlikely that the appellate courts were successful in catching all of the wrongful death sentences and reversing them, especially since the Supreme Court and the AEDPA had placed strict limitations on habeas corpus. The notion that states could be improperly executing innocent citizens is troubling in the abstract, but the sensational findings of the Columbia University studies became public around the same time that reports were emerging of malfunctioning death penalty systems across the nation. Illinois's Governor George Ryan declared a moratorium on that state's executions in 2000, following the revelation that investigations conducted by Northwestern University journalism students resulted in 13 exonerations.[1] Three years later, Ryan commuted the sentences of every death-row inmate, stating "that no matter how efficient and fair the death penalty may seem in theory, in actual practice it is primarily inflicted upon the weak, the poor, the ignorant and against racial minorities" (*New York Times* 2003).[2] Similar scenarios have played out in other parts of the country, as well. The state of Maryland authorized statistical examination of the racial and geographic distribution of its death sentences between 1978 and 1999. The research identified significant racial disparities, with black offenders most likely to face execution when their victims were white; it was concluded, "white decision makers in the capital punishment system may, therefore, unconsciously make decisions that favor white victims" (Paternoster et al. 2004:49).[3]

The idea that discriminatory death sentencing patterns exist without any discernable bigoted intent to produce them by law enforcement, prosecutors, jurors, and other relevant actors is noteworthy because it suggests that racial bifurcations are a natural by-product of discretionary judgments within the justice system. People are, in other words, socialized to respond in ways that produce and perpetuate unfairness even when striving for colorblind equality. There is perhaps no better illustration of this reality than Troy Davis being executed in 2009 despite an overwhelming lack of clarity about his actual role in the crime that landed him on death row. Davis was convicted in 1991 of murdering the off-duty police officer Mark McPhail, who at the time of his death was attempting to stop the assault of a homeless man in the parking lot of a Burger King restaurant where he was working as a security guard. At Davis's original trial, nine eyewitnesses testified to seeing him fire the gun, although it was unclear that any of them could have made a reasonable identification since the shooting occurred in the middle of the night and all were a considerable distance from the crime scene. The prosecutor claimed that Davis was recognizable due to his white shirt and that his accomplice, Sylvester "Redd" Coles, who participated in the assault but not the murder, had been wearing a yellow shirt. Circumstantial evidence was also presented that Davis had bragged to friends and a jailhouse informant about how he had killed McPhail. But Davis never confessed to police; he insisted that Coles was the actual shooter. Also, police never recovered the murder weapon, and there was no physical or DNA evidence implicating Davis in the crime. Ballistics evidence from recovered bullets, however, did connect him to the gun used to kill McPhail.

While none of these concerns were sufficient to acquit Davis of the crime, the facts underlying the eyewitness identifications and police conduct painted a disturbing picture. One of the eyewitnesses testified that she was near-sighted and not wearing her glasses when the crime happened. Another claimed at an appellate hearing that he ducked when the bullets were fired and only identified Davis as the shooter because he had seen his face on a wanted poster; while still another admitted to pinpointing Davis only after seeing him associated with the crime in a television news report. Several other eyewitnesses indicated that they were pressured and coerced by police. In one case, 16-year-old Darrell Collins alleged that officers threatened to charge him as an accessory to the McPhail murder if he failed to identify Davis as the murderer. The jailhouse informant, Kevin McQueen, admitted during a federal appellate hearing that he had lied in court because prosecutors had offered a favorable deal if he testified against Davis. Another acquaintance of Davis, Jeffrey Sapp, later admitted that police threatened him into testifying that Davis confessed to him about his guilt (see *In re Davis* (2010)).

Police and the prosecution vehemently denied the allegations of misconduct, but during the two decades of appeals that followed, questions about their actions in securing Davis's conviction and death sentence continued to mount. By the time Davis's legal team filed a habeas petition claiming evidence existed of his innocence, seven of nine eyewitnesses had recanted their testimony against Davis, while other witnesses now implicated Coles as the actual killer.[4] The Supreme Court ordered the habeas claim be reviewed by the District Court for the Southern District of Georgia, despite Antonin Scalia (joined by Clarence Thomas) channeling *Herrera v. Collins* (1993) in dissenting that it is not unconstitutional to execute "a convicted defendant who has had a full and fair trial but is later able to convince a habeas court that he is 'actually' innocent" (*In re Davis*, 557 U.S. 952, 955 (2009)). In 2010, the district court upheld the conviction and denied Davis's habeas writ. After being refused a hearing by the Eleventh Circuit Court of Appeals, Davis ultimately had his final appeal to the Supreme Court rejected and was executed on September 21, 2011, at the Georgia Diagnostic and Classification Prison. It was the same facility where Warren McCleskey had been put to death 20 years earlier.

Seeking Legislative Remedies

Events such as those surrounding the Troy Davis execution and rising numbers of inmates being exonerated from death row fueled the growing moratorium and abolition movements. More and more states began halting their death penalties—either practically by law or symbolically through disuse—and the number of offenders sentenced to death and executed declined significantly (see figure 5.1). Even the Rehnquist Court, which had contributed so prominently to the upsurge in executions during the 1990s, started narrowing the scope of capital punishment in landmark rulings such as *Atkins v. Virginia* (2002) and *Roper v. Simmons* (2005), which invalidated the death penalty for mentally retarded and juvenile offenders, respectfully.[5] By this time, Sandra Day O'Connor, who had voted with the majority in *McCleskey v. Kemp*, publicly stated that "serious questions are being raised" about the death penalty and perhaps ironically drew on statistical data in speculating about the likelihood of wrongful executions (Lane 2001; *New York Times* 2001).

The concerns expressed by O'Connor played a role in prompting several unsuccessful efforts to enact a federal Racial Justice Act during the 1990s (Arnold 2005; O. Johnson 2007; Vito and Higgins 2016), including a failed 1991 Senate bill intended to "reverse the Supreme Court's holding in *McCleskey v. Kemp*" (Posner and Spiro 1993:1222). Two states, however, subsequently passed their own statewide Racial Justice Acts. Kentucky became the first in 1998, after evidence of capital sentencing discrimination based on the race of defendants and victims was identified (see *Advocate* 1998).

The mechanics of the Act as approved are straightforward. At a pretrial conference, a defendant may allege that the prosecutor is seeking the death penalty on the basis of race. The defendant must present evidence showing that racial considerations played a significant part in the prosecution's decision to seek death in his case. Such evidence may include statistical evidence or other evidence that a death sentence was sought significantly more frequently either upon persons of one race than upon persons of another race, or as punishment for capital offenses against persons of one race than as punishment for capital offenses against persons of another race. The court will then schedule a hearing on the claim, and declare a time for the submission of evidence by the parties. At the hearing, the defendant bears the burden of proving by clear and convincing evidence that race was the basis of the Commonwealth's decision to seek the death penalty. The Commonwealth can offer rebuttal evidence. Finally, if the court finds that race was a basis of the decision to seek death, the court must order that a death sentence cannot be sought in that case. (Arnold 2005:103)

Thomas Keil and Gennaro Vito (2006) subsequently determined that Kentucky prosecutors are more likely to seek capital punishment in cases where the defendant is black and the victim is white. More recently, however, Jeffrey Kirchmeier suggests that Kentucky's Racial Justice Act has allowed the state to become "more even-handed in applying the death penalty in black victim and white victim cases," despite the fact that it "requires defendants to meet a high burden and link the evidence to the individual capital defendant in the case" (2015:276). In fact, the Kentucky law has been critizied for being too restrictive because it applies only to prosecutorial charging decisions and requires defendants to present a claim prior to the start of their criminal trial (R. Alexander 2014).

Following Kentucky's lead, in 2009 North Carolina similarly passed a Racial Justice Act, which allowed the admission of statistical data as evidence that race was a *significant* factor in death sentencing decisions. The principal basis of North Carolina's law was Isaac Unah's detailed empirical analysis of the state's capital punishment system. Modeled after the Baldus study (David Baldus and Jack Boger even served as consultants), Unah's study used complex statistical modeling to examine "capital punishment as a political process consisting of sequential decisions by the prosecutor and jury" that function as "several *interconnecting*, rather than independent, stages of analysis" (Unah 2011:613, emphasis in original). From this perspective, sentencing outcomes result from a complex and nuanced interplay between state actors, courtroom personnel, and citizen jurors "that is infused with highly conditional decision-making procedures" and incorporates a variety of "legal, institutional, and sociostructural conditions" (654). Among Unah's most prominent findings is the revelation that "race remains in essence a nonstatutory aggravating factor" in capital cases, meaning jurors either overtly or subconsciously ascribe greater culpability to nonwhite defendants. Unah therefore concluded that "race of victim *still* exerts a significant amount of influence in determining which homicide defendant lives or dies," despite also finding that "prosecutors are not exhibiting racially conscious tendencies in their decision to seek the death penalty" (654, emphasis in original).

Unah's research proved momentous because he showed that race was affecting sentencing outcomes in North Carolina even when prosecutors and jurors were not acting with any sort of biased intent. The very premise flies in the face of the Supreme Court's ruling in *McCleskey v. Kemp*, which mandated the finding of intentional discrimination as the

necessary burden of proof to establish a constitutional violation; and it influenced legislators to ratify a racial-justice
statute that did not require petitioners to provide proof of
discriminatory purpose. Instead, simply identifying the existence of racial disparities resulting from systemic factors
could have been sufficient to "establish a *prima facie* case of
substantial racial differences" in prosecutorial decisions to
seek or a jury's choice to impose the death penalty (Stiegel
2010:4, see also R. Alexander 2014). To meet this threshold,
petitioners were required to satisfy at least one of three conditions: "Death sentences were generally sought or imposed
upon one race more frequently, death sentences were sought
or imposed as punishment for capital offenses for one race
more frequently, or race was a considerable factor in peremptory challenges" (Stiegel 2010:4). The law's extensive protections against prosecutorial use of peremptory challenges
were particularly meaningful because they extended beyond
Batson requirements and allowed statistical evidence of discriminatory challenges to establish that race significantly
impacted the state's determination to seek death (see R. Alexander 2014).

Much broader in scope than the Kentucky law, North
Carolina's Racial Justice Act generated considerable controversy because it established a lower statutory standard to determine the existence of racial discrimination than the direct
proof of intent requirement mandated in *McCleskey* (Kotch
and Mosteller 2010). Accordingly, statistical evidence revealing sentencing or jury selection disparities in the county or
district where death was being sought or imposed was potentially sufficient for defendants to show that prosecutors,
judges, or jurors in their cases were significantly affected by
race regardless of whether they meant to discriminate. Although the state was entitled to rebut any evidence of racial

influence presented by the petitioner with its own statistical data, critics argued that the law was too defendant friendly and placed undue burdens on prosecutors, who were forced to divert attention away from their cases in order to address frivolous discovery requests (Kotch and Mosteller 2010; Kirchmeier 2015). North Carolina state senator Thom Goolsby articulated these concerns when he proclaimed that judges and prosecutors were inherently trustworthy but people should be skeptical about the motives of statisticians (Binker and Leslie 2012).

Even though identified violations of North Carolina's law only resulted in defendants' death sentences being reduced to life imprisonment without the possibility of parole, legislators swiftly moved to weaken the law by restricting the use of statistical data after nearly all of the state's death-row inmates filed Racial Justice Act claims (see Severson 2013). In the first case to be heard under the new law, Judge Greg Weeks ruled in favor of petitioner Marcus Raymond Robinson, who cited research conducted by Catherine M. Grosso and Barbara O'Brien (2012) that found that North Carolina prosecutors struck 52.6 percent of eligible black jurors via peremptory challenge, as compared to 25.7 percent of all other eligible jurors. The Robinson ruling sparked political backlash and fears of mass commutations that would delegitimize the state's entire criminal justice system. North Carolina's Conference of District Attorneys promptly issued a statement reading, "Capital cases reflect the most brutal and heinous offenders in our society. Whether the death penalty is an appropriate sentence for murderers should be addressed by our lawmakers in the General Assembly, not masked as claims (of) racism in our courts" (Baptiste 2017). Outraged conservative lawmakers rushed to amend the law; their revisions went into effect in 2012, after the state legislature overrode a gubernatorial veto. Among the changes, petitioners were now barred from presenting statewide or regional data and instead limited to statistical evidence from the jurisdiction where the crime occurred. Additionally, a stronger burden of proof was implemented. Statistical studies alone were no longer sufficient to have a death sentence commuted. Defendants were instead obliged to prove that their particular cases were uniquely harmed by racial considerations in a manner similar to the requirements established in *McCleskey*. State representative Paul Stam, who spearheaded the reform efforts, defended the changes by arguing that justice "is about individuals, not groups" (Binker and Leslie 2012).

Severely weakened by these reforms and a hostile political climate that was exacerbated when the Republican Party gained control of the state's General Assembly in 2012 and Democratic Governor Beverley Purdue decided not to seek reelection, North Carolina's Racial Justice Act was repealed in its entirety in 2013. But its legacy and impact persist. By 2014, Judge Greg Weeks ruled in favor of three other death-row inmates and commuted their sentences to life in prison without the possibility of parole. In addition, most of the more than 150 appeals filed prior to the repeal of the Racial Justice Act are still pending, albeit unlikely to ever receive a hearing given the law's repeal (see Blythe 2015). As for Marcus Raymond Robinson, his successful appeal has not turned out to be much of a victory.

Even though the law was still in effect when the four inmates' sentences were reduced, they weren't safe from death row just yet. Robinson's sentence had been legally reduced, but the legal battle was just beginning. In 2015, after nearly two years from the initial hearing, the North Carolina Supreme Court ordered the Superior Court to reconsider the reduced sen-

tences for Robinson, Augustine, Golphin, and Walters, saying the judge failed to give the state enough time to prepare
for the "complex" proceeding. This past January, Superior
Court Judge Erwin Spainhour ruled that because the RJA
had been repealed, the four defendants could no longer use
the law to reduce their sentences. . . . Robinson is back on
death row at Central Prison in the state's capital of Raleigh.
(Baptiste 2017)[6]

Robinson's return to death row and the short-lived existence of the North Carolina Racial Justice Act demonstrated
that public officials lacked the political will to confront the
extent to which racism is entrenched in the justice system.
Whether the decision to repeal the Racial Justice Act was
a matter of expedience or not wanting to appear soft on
crime is irrelevant to the fact that North Carolina legislators—in a manner similar to the Supreme Court majority
in *McCleskey*—ultimately decided that it is easier to execute
death-row inmates than to undergo the difficult transforma-
tive process needed to address the existence of discriminatory
capital sentencing outcomes.

Interpreting the Logic of Lewis Powell

The cultural and political backlash that seems to coincide
with efforts to pursue justice is a powerful reminder of the
"uncertainty about whether the past is really past, over and
concluded, or whether it continues, albeit in different forms
perhaps" (Said 1994:3). Historical racial divisions in the
United States, manifested visibly in the overrepresentation of
black Americans as the victims of lynching and foci of both
the pre- and post-*Furman* death penalty, reflect this point,
as does enduring support of capital punishment despite

conclusive evidence that it fails to deter crime and costs taxpayers considerably more than simply sentencing offenders to prison. In Georgia alone, the abolition of slavery was met with the creation of a convict-lease system (1868) using state prisoners who were overwhelmingly black in composition, a statewide poll tax (1877), and white primary elections (1908) at the behest of Governor Hoke Smith, who also enacted a literacy test and property-ownership voting restrictions. In Atlanta, Mayor William B. Hartsfield barred the hiring of black American police officers prior to 1948, after which they were segregated at the Butler Street YMCA, patrolled only black neighborhoods, and were prohibited from arresting a white person until 1969 (Mason 2000).[7] The Georgia legislature further attempted through the Sibley Commission of 1955 to defund school districts choosing to follow federal law and integrate student bodies in the wake of *Brown v. Board of Education of Topeka* (1954); and Georgia's antimiscegenation statutes prohibited interracial marriage until *Loving v. Virginia* forced a change in 1967 (see Carson 1981). It was in specific response to *Brown v. Board of Education* that Governor Herman Talmadge articulated the state's official stance on segregation, noting, "the people of Georgia believe in, adhere to, and will fight for their rights . . . to manage their own affairs" and "will not tolerate the mixing of races in the public schools or any of its tax-supported institutions" (1955:56).

Bearing in mind the stubborn resistance Georgia exhibited to any advancement for black Americans from the end of the Civil War until the late 1960s, when explicit segregation would have precipitated federal intervention, it becomes clear that the blatant discrimination of "the past" was indeed a very recent past (Harmon 1996). It was this enduring epitaph of U.S. justice that Jack Boger so candidly articulated before the Supreme Court in stating, "the old habits of mind, the racial attitudes of that time have survived . . . into the current century" (*McCleskey*, No. 84-6811, at 0:57). If anything, the Baldus study quantified just how profoundly racial considerations continued to affect the legal process in Georgia, notwithstanding the supposed safeguards put in place to ensure super due process following *Gregg* and the reinstitution of capital punishment in 1976.[8] When contrasted with Mary Beth Westmoreland's mostly unsubstantiated assertions that black murders are qualitatively different from white murders—an argument that failed to even address the race of victim effect, which primarily indicated the likelihood of a death sentence in any given case—a fascinating picture emerged of how the majority justices interpreted the constitutional relevance of empirical data indicating systemic racial sentencing disparities. Lewis Powell's personal jurisprudence is especially noteworthy because he ruled against McCleskey despite acknowledging that "there can be no perfect procedure for deciding in which cases governmental authority should be used to impose death" (*McCleskey*, 481 U.S. at 313).

It is perhaps unfair to expect any criminal proceedings, let alone those that authorize the state and federal governments to end the lives of their citizens, to be objectively unimpeded by some form of bias. Even if we concede the appropriateness of accommodating a degree of prejudice and other extralegal considerations into the capital process, Powell completely disregarded the existential threat to capital defendants posed by prosecutorial, judicial, and institutional misconduct. In fact, he limited his consideration only to juror behavior during trial and sentencing deliberations and, even so, neglected to specify precisely what level or amount of racial prejudice influencing a jury's judgment breaches the threshold of constitutional unacceptability. Powell's failure to achieve clarity on this important point might be attributed to his efforts at weighing Georgia's claim to execute against the petitioner's right to due process and equal protection under the law. Paul W. Kahn (1987) observes that balancing the roles of social institutions with the needs and interests of the broader communities they serve was an integral part of Powell's jurisprudence. In *Furman*, for example, Powell expressed concern that judicial intrusion would divide a citizenry that largely favored the use of capital punishment by state governments elected to represent their interests.

To the extent we assume that communal values in Georgia generally favor a racially neutral death penalty, Powell's legal reasoning in *McCleskey* is somewhat confusing because he concluded that sentencing disparities, which have historically punished people of color more harshly than whites, are an inevitable part of the justice system. At the same time, Powell seemed to assume that discretionary judgments made by prosecutors, jurors, and other courtroom actors fail to pose a constitutional risk—notwithstanding Georgia's extensive legacy of racially motivated justice—unless purposeful discrimination is identified in individual cases. Even though Powell was correct in asserting that the Baldus study fails to empirically prove the existence of intentional prejudice, the racialized sentencing discrepancies he described as inexorable have remained fundamentally unchanged since the time of slavery, convict-lease, and Jim Crow and despite every attempt at civil rights advancement. Rather than accede to this undeniable historical truth, Powell praised reform efforts for minimizing racial discrimination to levels of constitutional irrelevance: "Because of the risk that the factor of race may enter the criminal justice process, we have engaged in 'unceasing efforts' to eradicate racial prejudice from our criminal justice system" (*McCleskey*, 481 U.S. at 309). To a degree,

Powell was correct. Despite the racist heritage of social life in Georgia, discriminatory capital sentencing outcomes do not reflect the shared conscience of most contemporary Georgians. Nevertheless, Powell appeared to simply trust that human actors who have collectively proven themselves incapable of purging both conscious and unintended racial animus from social institutions could realize a truly equitable justice system.

Setting aside the fact that the Baldus study conclusively demonstrated that none of the problems identified in *Furman* had been corrected (or even moderately improved on) by all of the reforms enacted by *Gregg*, critical race scholarship instructs that racism *is the status quo* in U.S. society. Specifically, it is the casual everyday forms of prejudice often overlooked by the unaffected that commonly produce the unfair and disparate outcomes identified in capital sentencing and other areas of social life, such as drug-law enforcement, criminal profiling, segregated schooling, and financial redlining of poor urban neighborhoods (see Delgado and Stefancic 2012). Studies dating back to 1977, for instance, have found that overtly discriminatory obstacles to prevent blacks, Hispanics, Latinx, and Asian Americans from securing adequate housing are not nearly as prevalent as more discreet forms of bias, such as predatory lending practices, charging minority tenants higher rent, and maneuvering nonwhites toward less desirable neighborhoods (see Dewan 2013:B3). The point is, despite Powell's contention that unceasing reform efforts in the post-civil-rights era have effectively eliminated the constitutional risk of racial prejudice in capital sentencing, these subtler forms of discrimination continue to flourish, in part, because they invoke discretionary judgments. Hence, just as realtors can choose to show more houses in better areas and quote lower prices to prospective white buyers, "the law gives prosecutors complete discretion either to seek a death sentence in death-eligible cases or to waive the death penalty—unilaterally or by way of a negotiated plea bargain. For cases that advance to a penalty trial, the typical jury exercises virtually complete discretion on the life or death decision once it finds a statutory aggravating circumstance present in the case. In addition, the governor or board of pardons and parole generally has complete discretion to commute a death sentence to either life without possibility of parole or a term of years" (Baldus et al. 1998:1644). On this matter, Powell merely supposes that discretion benefits defendants because prosecutors, jurors, and other justice officials have the power to be lenient; that is, they can sentence offenders to a less severe punishment instead of invoking the death penalty.

While it is true "the power to be lenient [also] is the power to discriminate" (*McCleskey*, 481 U.S. at 312), Powell's rationalization is a bit perplexing considering that the Baldus study demonstrates that discretionary decisions by jurors are often influenced by racial considerations. Regardless of how or why such a conclusion was reached in the face of empirical evidence that black defendants are habitually—and perhaps purposefully—sentenced more harshly in capital cases, Powell's reasoning fundamentally contradicts the death penalty reforms established in *Gregg*, which were intended to ensure uniformity in capital sentencing, as well as to establish super due process to guard against the dissimilar treatment of offenders during the sentencing phase. The result was a Court ruling that condoned racism in the legal process, perhaps because confronting "the reality of racial influence on death sentences would risk disturbing the system too much" (Lewis 1987:A31).

To infer that Supreme Court justices would sidestep the Baldus study and uphold Warren McCleskey's death sentence simply because doing so was easier than confronting systemic bias that debases the entire justice system would be unfathomable if Powell had not made that very point in his majority opinion.

> McCleskey's claim, taken to its logical conclusion throws into serious question the principles that underlie our entire justice system. . . . Thus, if we accepted McCleskey's claim that racial bias has impermissibly tainted the capital sentencing decision, we could soon be faced with similar claims as to other types of penalty. Moreover, that claim that his sentence rests on the irrelevant factor of race easily could be extended to apply to claims based on unexplained discrepancies that correlate to membership in other minority groups, and even to gender. Similarly, since McCleskey's claim relates to the race of his victim, other claims could apply with equally logical force to statistical disparities that correlate with the race or sex of other actors in the criminal justice system, such as defense attorneys or judges. (*McCleskey*, 481 U.S. at 314–317)

Justice Brennan addressed Powell's reasoning in his dissent, writing that the majority was concerned "that recognition of McCleskey's claim would open the door to widespread challenges to all aspects of criminal sentencing," which seemed "to suggest a fear of too much justice" (*id.* at 339).

The Subtle Menace of Colorblind Racism

Considering the Court's *McCleskey* ruling in light of the Baldus study's findings, it is worth questioning whether the so-called transformations brought about by the civil rights movement made any significant changes in the criminal justice operations of Georgia and the United States more generally. Jack Boger certainly implied that capital sentencing disparities extended from pervasive flaws in Georgia's justice system that systematically maltreated minority suspects and defendants, beginning with police questioning, including the conduct of prosecutors, and extending to the circumstances of incarceration. It has become fashionable in the post-civil-rights United States to romanticize about chimeras of whites and blacks living side by side in harmony while reducing all instances of bigotry and racial inequality, be they historical, psychological, or statistical, to being the products of overt hate. Peeling aside this façade, a prima facie case for the consistent and continuing institutional degradation of people of color in Georgia exists. Georgians were enthusiastic supporters of slavery and convict-lease, which exploited the Thirteenth Amendment's provision that involuntary servitude was permissible "as a punishment for crime whereof the party shall have been duly convicted." Freedmen were arrested en masse and then leased out for a small fee to private farmers and businesspeople, for whom they effectively labored during the day as slaves. Whereas slave owners had incentive to sustain modest accommodations for the health and welfare of their property, leased convicts were cheaply acquired, easily replaced, and subject to unspeakably inhumane treatment. Meekly protective slave codes were replaced by the Reconstruction Amendments that prescribed Black Codes and eventually Jim Crow laws that limited the autonomy of newly freed slaves and reaffirmed their "blackness" by enforcing measures such as labor discipline, movement restrictions, and antimiscegenation.

Although convict-lease was finally abolished in 1928, many of these limitations and prohibitions remained in force until the late 1960s and were only involuntarily removed from legal codes, a fact reflective of cultural attitudes preserving second-class citizenship for black Americans. In seems unlikely that such powerful and long-tenured institutional racism was wiped out between 1968, when restrictions on intermarriage were struck down, and 1973, when Georgia resumed death sentencing under its revised post-*Furman* law. In truth, the nature and practice of racism has evolved from a brute to a symbolic genocide that for all practical purposes was crystallized when the Supreme Court failed to recognize—or willfully disregarded—how the Baldus study revealed a justice system cloaked by a culture of systemic bias and structural racism. Manifestations of discrimination are all too evident in U.S. social life, from racial profiling and the disproportionate use of force by law enforcement against (unarmed) black Americans[9] to motorists being less likely to yield for people of color at intersections (Vedantam 2017) and even to the Flint, Michigan, water crisis, which a government-appointed civil rights commission determined to be caused by "historical, structural and systemic racism combined with implicit bias" (Almasy and Ly 2017; see also Michigan Civil Rights Commission 2017).

Perhaps because the precise causes and sources of institutionalized discrimination are difficult to visualize, a considerable number of white Americans tend to disavow the possibility that people of color experience racial disadvantage (see Hill 2008) and in some instances believe that the real crisis is *reverse racism* that victimizes whites. The problem is not that Americans are insensitive to prejudice; a majority of the population views racial discrimination as a pressing social problem (Thompson and Clement 2016). Instead, there is a tacit cultural acceptance of subtle, laissez-faire bigotry that does not result from discriminatory intent, per se, but rather from white civil society persistently stereotyping people of color and erecting barriers that restrict the economic, political, and social progress of black men and women, who are then blamed if they fail to achieve a white middle-class standard of living. From this perspective, black criminality is not punished more harshly because of racial hatred. To the contrary, laissez-faire bias is colorblind and sterilized of any identifiable racist assumptions. Black offenders are simply framed as rational actors who have personally failed, whether due to false assumptions of laziness, unwillingness to abide by social norms, incapacity for self-improvement, or not taking advantage of social programs such as affirmative action that elevate racial minorities above whites (see Bobo, Kluegel, and Smith 1997).

Racial stereotypes perpetuated by colorblind ideology and rhetoric undoubtedly fuel the paradoxical views of Americans who oppose discrimination while associating criminality with archetypal representations of young black men in urban environments (see J. Johnson 2007; Hetey and Eberhardt 2014; see also Maratea and Monahan 2014). Consider the fact that research indicates jurors perceive the physical attributes of black offenders as "powerful cues of deathworthiness" (Eberhardt et al. 2006:385).[10] *Looking black*, in other words, increases the likelihood a defendant will be sentenced to death. Bobo and Smith attribute these stereotypical responses to an inherent moral conflict among whites who cherish the "the values of freedom, individual rights, democracy, equality, and justice" (1998:183) while holding negative attitudes toward blacks whom they believe do not work hard enough to achieve meaningful personal and collective progress. Polling data tend to support this perspective, indicating that a considerable number of white Americans view blacks as less intelligent, lacking in work ethic, and lagging behind whites due to a lack of motivation (ANES 2016; Blake 2017; Flitter and Kahn 2016). A much smaller percentage feels that people of color "are treated less fairly than whites" in the public sphere (Pew Research Center 2016).

The "kindler, gentler, antiblack ideology" of laissez-faire racism cultivates ongoing racial inequality through persistent negative labeling of blacks even while U.S. society attempts to root out pernicious forms of discrimination and promote greater equality (Bobo, Kluegel, and Smith 1997:15; see also Bobo and Smith 1998). When viewed through this lens, the maltreatment of disenfranchised minority defendants is admittedly difficult to rectify because the legal statutes that guide often well-intentioned prosecutors, judges, and jurors are race neutral in appearance. Anyone seeking to mount a legal challenge of post-*Gregg* capital punishment statutes is thus burdened with the task of showing discriminatory purpose where there appears to be none. For petitioners such as Warren McCleskey, the precedent established in *Yick Wo v. Hopkins* (1886) provides a potential pathway for advancing equal protection and due process claims. In *Yick Wo*, the Supreme Court declared unconstitutional a San Francisco ordinance requiring laundry facilities not located in brick or stone buildings to receive approval from the city's board of supervisors. Although the ordinance made no mention of race or ethnicity, the Court determined that it was administered in a discriminatory fashion because enforcement was targeted almost exclusively against Chinese-owned laundries, many of which were located in wooden buildings (see Failinger 2012). In a unanimous opinion, Justice Stanley Matthews described public officials as applying the law in an "unequal and oppressive" manner that deprived Chinese laundry owners of equal protection, "whatever may have been the intent of the ordinance as adopted" (*Yick Wo v. Hopkins*, 118 U.S. 356, 373 (1886)). "Though the law itself be fair on its face and impartial in appearance," Justice Matthews further reasoned, "if it is applied and administered by public authority with an evil eye and an unequal hand, so as practically to make unjust and illegal discriminations between persons in similar circumstances, material to their rights, the denial of equal justice is still within the prohibition of the Constitution" (*id.* at 373–374).

Unlike *Yick Wo*, the federal courts in *McCleskey v. Kemp* never determined that the application of Georgia's post-*Gregg* capital statutes *so exclusively* targeted black defendants as to constitute an equal protection violation. Between 1977 and 1999, there were 243 death-row inmates in Georgia, of which 114 were black (46.9 percent). While that number was disproportionate to the racial distribution of the state's entire population, which was about 27 percent black between 1980 and 1990, it was considerably less than the black proportion of the total inmate population (72.1 percent) during those years (Blume, Eisenberg, and Wells 2004). The heightened percentage of white offenders on death row as compared to the general prison population functioned as a sort of *racial ballast* that legitimized the veneer of race neutrality in capital sentencing and insulated the state against claims of disparate treatment (intentional discrimination) and disparate impact (a disproportionately adverse effect). The affectation of racial ballast in determining those who are deserving execution illustrates the reality of guided discretion at work in Georgia. Whereas the elimination of Jim Crow made statutory, racially ascribed discrimination illegal, the pronounced motives of the Supreme Court in attempting to narrow the class of offenders eligible for death have had a somewhat curious effect. In addition to black Americans, who remain the prime candidates for condemnation, a host of white offenders have been added to states' death rows notwithstanding the underlying fact that only 20 white homicide offenders have, in the post-*Furman* era, been executed for taking the life of a black American (as compared to 288 executions of black offenders for taking the life of a white victim) (Death Penalty Information Center 2018).[11]

If nothing else, racial ballast signifies that states have succeeded in symbolically diluting the pool of death-eligible offenders, whose complexion has become somewhat lighter since *Gregg*. However, the fact remains that federal safeguards enacted to protect against racial bias have mostly succeeded in permitting prosecutors and juries to reach racially loaded results without openly discriminating.[12] When considered alongside the Court's ruling that statistical evidence such as the Baldus study is functionally irrelevant to establishing equal protection and due process violations in capital cases, petitioners such as Warren McCleskey face bleak prospects. After all, McCleskey's entire case attempted to demonstrate that "a double standard for sentencing" resulted from "the Georgia system [allowing] for an impermissible value judgment by the actors within the system—that white life is more valuable than black life" (*Zant*, 580 F. Supp. at 348). If empirical research inferring discrimination based on general sentencing patterns offers nothing of value to a given case and no courtroom actors verbally express racist beliefs or intent during trial, then petitioners such as McCleskey cannot possibly call into question the "integrity, propriety, or fairness" of statewide capital sentencing practices (*id.* at 348). As a matter of pragmatic observation, there has been a litany of legal challenges to the fundamental equity of innumerable aspects of the criminal justice system, including the death penalty. Since reinstatement with *Gregg* introduced the requirement that aggravating factors be present for an offender to be death eligible, capital punishment has been tinkered with extensively and limited considerably in scope to further restrict its application in practice (see Goldstone 2009). States are no longer permitted to execute minors under the age of 18 (*Roper v. Simmons* (2005)), offenders deemed intellectually disabled or too incompetent at the time of execution (*Atkins v. Virginia* (2002); *Ford v. Wainwright* (1986)), rapists (*Coker v. Georgia* (1977)), or anyone who committed a crime that has not directly resulted in the victim's death (*Kennedy v. Louisiana* 2008).[13] Taken in totality, these narrowing efforts have intended to eliminate the vestiges of arbitrary and capricious death sentencing that were identified in *Furman* and to ensure that only the most deserving are executed (Sharon 2011).

Capital Sentencing, Proportionality, and Race in Georgia

Setting aside any systemic flaws in Georgia's legal process and ongoing efforts to perfect capital punishment practices by restricting its usage, there remains the question of whether Warren McCleskey's death sentence was comparable to sentences for other crimes with similar aggravation. *Proportionality of sentence* is regularly invoked by appellants and abolitionists and is often denigrated by public officials when defending their intents and motives for carrying out an execution. The death penalty is at its most basic supposed to be reserved for the proverbial *worst-of-the-worst* offenders and not necessarily applied to all homicide cases. For this reason, only a small number of eligible defendants should ever be sentenced to death row and each for a crime of comparable severity. In chapter 3, it was mentioned that the state of Georgia argued in *Furman* that the relative disuse of capital punishment was the result of a strategic practice of informed selectivity, whereby proper safeguards were implemented to ensure that only the most deserving offenders were executed.

William Brennan dismissed this claim outright by reasoning, "when the rate of infliction is at [such a] low level, it is highly implausible that only the worst criminals or the criminals who commit the worst crimes are selected for punishment" (*Furman*, 408 U.S. at 294). His argument was twofold. First, he posited that no state implemented a rational procedure for differentiating the small number of offenders sentenced to death from all of the other murderers who simply got prison sentences.[14] Second, Brennan challenged Georgia's contention that capital punishment has a moralizing effect by pointing out a logical flaw in the state's reasoning: if the death penalty serves a social benefit and reflects the values of the citizenry, a policy of informed selectivity is counterproductive because it diminishes those effects (*Furman*, 408 U.S. at 294–295, 303). Simply put, a far greater number of offenders would need to be executed in order to maximize its moralizing and protective benefits; but in doing so, states would have to abandon any guise of informed selectivity.

At the heart of Brennan's challenge endures a fundamental truth. The question of whether the state has a legitimate right to kill its citizens is philosophically bound to a long-standing moral, ethical, and legal conundrum: is the right to life absolute, or are there instances when a given offender's conduct is so heinous that it results in a forfeiture of the right to life? Thurgood Marshall spoke to this idea when he noted that even the most ardent death penalty supporters do not favor purposeless vengeance enacted without just reason and thoughtful consideration (*Furman*, 408 U.S. at 363). His assertion is axiomatic in that decisions to execute, and punish more generally, reflect a shared humanism; they compel us to discipline those who violate the welfare of others but not to sentence offenders to death simply because their crimes elicit sufficient moral outrage to surmise that they *deserve* to die.

Undoubtedly there is an element of truth to Marshall's suggestion that punishment reflects a community's shared values when authorized with a sense of purpose and morality, which he found lacking in capital punishment. Marshall therefore believed that if the "great mass of citizens" were properly informed that "it is usually the poor, the illiterate, the underprivileged, the member of the minority group—the man who, because he is without means, and is defended by a court-appointed attorney—who becomes society's sacrificial lamb" and of the existing "evidence that innocent people have been executed before their innocence can be proved," then they "would conclude . . . that the death penalty is immoral and therefore unconstitutional" (*Furman*, 408 U.S. at 363–364).

The problem with Marshall's hypothesis is that most Americans cite retribution as the primary reason they support the death penalty (Swift 2014). Rooted in the *eye for an eye* code of justice, retribution means that the punishment fits the crime and is achieved when the offender is sanctioned to as equivalent a degree as possible to the harm inflicted on the victim. From a retributivist perspective, the death penalty is morally justified because an execution would correspond in severity to the injury that resulted from illegally taking a life. To the degree that the laws guiding the use of capital punishment appear to be racially neutral and applied with informed selectivity by prosecutors and jurors, then, there is no moral conundrum to whether executing is appropriate so long as members of a citizenry view the death penalty as successfully achieving the goal of legally authorized retaliation (known as the principle of *lex talionis*). Murderers are put to death because they deserve to die for taking the life of an innocent victim. Unfortunately, retributivist justifications for capital punishment are not so cut-and-dry and therefore inherently problematic because there is an incon-

TABLE 5.1. Georgia Legal Executions, by Race, 1735–2016

Race	Pre-*Furman*		Post-*Furman*	
	Executions before 1900	Executions 1900–1972	Executions 1976–2016	Victims of executed offenders 1976–2016
Black	210	511	23	9
White	96	112	42	81
Other	17	2	—	—
Total	323	625	65	90

Source: Death Penalty Information Center 2017b, 2017c

sistency between retributivist philosophical intent and the practical functioning of the death penalty. Most killers are not executed, which means that only a select few merit dying for their crimes, even though all murderers have purposely ended the life of another person. Furthermore, the notion that someone *deserves* to die does not imply a morally equivalent response drawn from a reasoned or rational notion of justice. It instead insinuates the desire for revenge, which is not a legally justified response to crime.

U.S. history is littered with evidence of retributive ideals being perverted to justify vengeful social-control practices that target people of color and the poor. W. E. B. DuBois wrote in *The Souls of Black Folks* that "the police system of the South was originally designed to keep track of all Negroes, not simply of criminals; and when the Negroes were freed, . . . the first and foremost universal device was to use the courts as a means of reënslaving the blacks" ([1903] 1989:145). DuBois's assertion is hardly a historical artifact. Of the 690 legal executions in Georgia since 1900, 534 involved black Americans offenders (77.4 percent), and a full 90 percent of victims in post-*Furman* execution cases through 2016 (81 of 90) were white (see table 5.1). These numbers reflect how ongoing racial bifurcation in Georgia's capital process follows a clear pattern of prioritizing the protection of white victims. Whereas the general characterization of the pre-*Furman* death penalty is as freakish, capricious, and without reason (*Furman*, 408 U.S. at 293), there certainly seems to be a discernable rationale behind who is selected for death in post-*Gregg* Georgia.

The More Things Change, the More They Stay the Same

Over the period 1876–1972, black Americans accounted for the vast majority of those who were lynched and executed in the state of Georgia. Based on the overwhelming frequency of mob lynching targeting black Americans and the proportion of pre-*Furman* legal executions having been imposed against black offenders (76 percent), the reform efforts in Georgia law authorized by *Gregg* in 1976 have succeeded in reducing this disparity. Through 2016, the post-*Furman* period has seen the percentage of black Americans executed by the state drop to 35 percent, alongside a corresponding increase in the ratio of white offenders put to death (see table 5.1). To a reasonable degree, capital sentences in Georgia appear to reflect the successful application of *Gregg*-mandated reforms. Yet the seeming racial recalibration of Georgia death sentencing masks the fact that capital punishment remains a profoundly flawed practice.

Although the courts and state legislatures continue to develop legal formulas and procedural changes to "tinker with the machinery of death" (*Callins v. Collins*, 510 U.S. 1141, 1145 (1994)), the racialized patterns and practice of capital punishment in the post-*Gregg* United States are remarkably similar to the pre-*Furman* era, bear a likeness to bifurcated Jim Crow justice, remain capricious and arbitrary in application (see

Donohue 2014), and are overwhelmingly concentrated in southern states that "also dominated lynchings and governmentally enforced racial segregation" (Zimring 2003:96). The issue at hand is not whether Warren McCleskey and other people of color on death row have received disparate punishment because legislators, prosecutors, judges, and jurors enacted, maintained, or implemented death penalty statutes for their anticipated discriminatory effect in order to contrive the *legal lynching* of black offenders. Rather, in *Gregg v. Georgia*, the Supreme Court determined and has continued to maintain in subsequent rulings that capital sentencing systems can operate in fair and neutral manners. There is indeed no compelling evidence that policy makers en masse act with discriminatory intent when ratifying and supporting capital punishment statutes, and state legislatures necessarily require wide discretion in the choice of criminal laws and penalties. But what the Baldus study and subsequent death penalty research have made clear is that profound racially disproportionate outcomes that uniquely harm economically poor, nonwhite criminal defendants persist despite every institutional effort to ensure that capital sentencing decisions are colorblind.

Conclusion

Past Is Prologue: Why McCleskey *Still Matters*

In 1987, the same year the Supreme Court ruled in *McCleskey v. Kemp*, a Texas jury sentenced Duane Buck to death for multiple murders, including the killing of his girlfriend in front of her daughter. Neither his lawyers nor supporters ever contested his guilt; Buck had most certainly committed the gruesome crimes. Yet his case sparked a protracted legal battle when on appeals Buck asserted that his Sixth Amendment right to a fair trial was violated and that he had been sentenced to death simply because he is black. The bulk of his claim rested on expert testimony provided during trial by the psychologist Walter Quijano, who informed jurors that Buck was more likely to commit additional crimes in the future because of his race, citing as proof "an over-representation of Blacks among violent offenders" (*Buck v. Davis*, 137 S. Ct. 759, 768 (2017)). Quijano's testimony was devastating because juries in Texas are only allowed to sentence an eligible offender to death in the event they determine that person is currently and will be in the future a continuing threat to society. On top of that, Quijano had actually been called to testify by the defense. During sentencing, the prosecutor exploited the incendiary statements, telling jurors, "you heard from Dr. Quijano, who had a lot of experience in the Texas Department of Corrections, who told you that there was a probability that the man would commit future acts of violence" (Fernandez 2011:A14).

Upon appeal, attorneys from the NAACP Legal Defense Fund took over Buck's case, arguing that it reflected the unavoidable presence of racial prejudice in the administration of capital punishment. In many ways, Quijano's testimony seemed to reflect the very sort of purposeful discrimination required to establish a constitutional violation, as determined by the Supreme Court in *McCleskey v. Kemp*. As is often the case, however, proving that Buck was actually harmed by racial bias during trial was no easy task. In 2009, the Fifth Circuit Court of Appeals asserted that Buck's death penalty should move forward because defense counsel was responsible for advancing Quijano's testimony. Although the Supreme Court later granted a stay in 2011, Buck's case was again rejected for a hearing on the basis that Quijano was appointed an expert witness by the defense. Justice Alito (joined by Scalia and Breyer) conceded that Quijano's testimony was "bizarre and objectionable" but determined that it would only provide a basis for reversal if the prosecution was responsible for the jury hearing those statements: "But Dr. Quijano was a defense witness, and it was petitioner's attorney, not the prosecutor, who first elicited Dr. Quijano's view regarding the correlation between race and future dangerousness" (Liptak 2016; see also Cohen 2011).

By 2013, more than 100 public officials, religious leaders, and lawyers had voiced their support for granting Buck a new hearing on the basis that race appeared to play a central role in his sentencing outcome. Complicating matters, however, was the fact that Quijano claimed his testimony lacked discriminatory intent because he merely articulated "statistical factors [known] to predict future dangerous," which include the race of offender. When asked by the defense to specifically discuss how racial factors affect the justice system, Quijano told the jury, "it is a sad commentary that minorities, Hispanics and black people, are overrepresented in the criminal justice system" (Chammah 2013; Rosenthal 2011). Furthermore, Quijano later clarified in an interview with the *Texas Tribune* that he never stated that Buck was a continuing threat to society, but rather his "statements about race were meant to show there was a 'relational' connection between race and dangerousness, and not a 'causal' connection" (Chammah 2013). At the very least, the intellectual complexities of that argument were perhaps lost on the jury, particularly after the prosecutor exploited the supposed linkage between race and future criminality during the sentencing hearing.

A full 30 years after Duane Buck was originally sentenced to death, a final resolution to his capital case has only recently been achieved. In 2015, the Fifth Circuit Court of Appeals again rejected the petitioner's appellate claim "that the state's failure to admit error and waive defenses was extraordinary and merited relief," while effectively sidestepping the question of whether race was (or should be) a determining factor in capital sentencing (*Buck v. Stephens*, 623 Fed. Appx. 668, 670 (5th Cir. 2015)). The Supreme Court nonetheless granted Buck a writ of certiorari in 2016; the decision was probably influenced by the state of Texas admitting to trial irregularities in seven other cases in which Quijano had provided testimony linking race to criminal violence. What made this revelation even more astonishing was that problems surrounding Quijano's courtroom statements had been exposed publicly 16 years earlier when Vincent Saldano had his death penalty vacated due to trial error. In that case, Quijano "suggested that Saldano should be executed because, as an Hispanic, he posed a special risk of future dangerousness to society. To support this astonishing conclusion, the expert pointed out that Hispanics make up a disproportionately large amount of Texas' prison population" (Lazarus 2000). The troubling nature of Quijano's claims during the Saldano trial sparked an investigation that led then–attorney general of Texas John Cornyn to acknowledge "eight other cases involving racial testimony by Quijano, six of which the AG said were similar to Saldano's case; one of those was Buck's" (*Buck*, 628 Fed. Appx. at 670).

Perhaps because Quijano's testimony during Buck's trial was solicited by the defense, the investigation somehow failed to identify or acknowledge error in his case, allowing the legal battle over Buck's execution to continue for another 17 years. In *Buck v. Davis* (2017), though, the Court ruled in a 6–2 decision that Quijano's testimony linking race and future criminality was unconstitutional even when introduced by defense counsel.[1] Writing for the majority, Chief Justice John Roberts described the strain of racial prejudice that tainted Duane Buck's trial as a toxin that "can be deadly in small doses" (*Buck*, 137 S. Ct. at 777). But Roberts was only referring to deliberate bias that leads to disparate treatment of minority defendants in capital cases and not the disparate impact of structural racism that corrupts the application of capital punishment. And Roberts's assertion that racial considerations are "a disturbing departure from a basic premise of our criminal justice system" (*id.* at 778) perhaps unintentionally speaks to the inherent difficulty in rooting out prejudice from capital sentencing because it reflects a patent denial that race and its associated biases have historically existed in symbiosis with the U.S. justice apparatus.

The Freakish Pursuit of Justice

If the Duane Buck case tells us anything, it is that Jack Boger's foundational assertion in *McCleskey v. Kemp* that the old habits of mind and racial attitudes of the past have survived in the present day. In Boger's attempt to sensitize the Court to the problem of institutional racism, he offered complex statistical data to demonstrate the post-*Gregg* persistence of discriminatory outcomes even when overtly identifiable bias is absent in any given death penalty case. His presentation of the Baldus study undercut the foundational rationale anchoring the Supreme Court's decision to reinstate capital punishment in *Gregg*: that bifurcating capital trials into distinct criminal and sentencing phases, implementing super due process during appellate phases, and employing statutory aggravating and mitigating circumstances that provide jurors with guided discretion would overcome the problems of arbitrary and racially discriminatory sentencing patterns in states such as Georgia. But there was no evidence then, and none now, that capital jurors separate sentencing decisions from their personal prejudices and racial biases. Potter Stewart argued in *Gregg* that when "left unguided, juries imposed the death sentence in a way that could only be called freakish. The new Georgia sentencing procedures, by contrast, focus the jury's attention on the particularized nature of the crime and the particularized characteristics of the individual defendant. . . . In this way the jury's discretion is channeled. No longer can a jury wantonly and freakishly impose the death sentence; it is always circumscribed by the legislative guidelines" (428 U.S. at 206–207). Justice Stewart assumed that jurors would reach individualized judgments based on informed perceptions of offenders' personal culpability, determined by balancing the aggravating factors in a given case against any possible mitigating circumstances. William Bowers, Benjamin Fleury-Steiner, and Michael Antonio argue that in *Penry v. Lynaugh*, the Court regarded capital sentencing decision as a reasoned moral choice because "the decision must be an 'individualized assessment' of the character and record of the particular offender and the circumstances of the particular offense, unencumbered by ignorance or emotion, and supported with information sufficient and relevant for reliable rational decision-making" (2003:415).

There are, of course, no mandates or guidance provided in the post-*Gregg* statutes in Georgia or any other state that can actually ensure that jurors tasked with subjectively determining the fate of a criminal offender will reach reliable sentencing decisions without being prejudiced, either consciously or unconsciously, by ignorance, emotion, race, or any other factor that may reasonably affect judgment—especially when the circumstances of a case are highly graphic and emotionally charged (see *Turner v. Murray* (1986)). In fact, the Supreme Court ruled in *Pena-Rodriguez v. Colorado* (2017) that secrecy in jury deliberations is limited when evidence exists of racial and ethnic bias. The petitioner's appellate grievance focused on a juror purportedly saying that the defendant was guilty of sexual assault "because he's Mexican and Mexican men take whatever they want" (137 S. Ct. 855, 862 (2017)). Justice Kennedy made clear in his majority opinion that "racial bias implicates unique historical, constitutional, and institutional concerns," but he also noted that "the promise of equal treatment under the law" is achieved through Court decisions that address "the most grave and serious statements of racial bias" (*id.* at 868).[2] The truth is that no court can legislate jurors' thoughts, personal sense of morality, or even their actual understanding of the statutory guidance provided them in a capital case unless overt statements of discriminatory intent or factual misunderstanding are made in the presence of fellow jurors or other court actors. The same is true for prosecutors, judges, expert witnesses, law enforcement personnel, and any other formal actors or institutional processes that may purposefully or unintentionally taint the capital process on the basis of subjective interpretation or how the law is applied on a case-by-case basis.

It is important never to overlook the fact that racial discrimination in the justice system "affects everything from arrest to voir dire to sentencing" and "has origins outside of the legal system that contribute to the failures within that system" (Parker, DeWees, and Radelet 2003:49). Prejudice and bigotry are so innately immersed in the cultural fabric of U.S. society that they negatively affect the justice system and disproportionately harm people of color and the poor even before the legal process is initiated. In many ways, Warren McCleskey's legal fate was *influenced* the day he was born by the complex and ever-present intersections of race with institutionalized inequality, structural discrimination, and laissez-faire prejudice, all of which affect the functioning of the criminal justice personnel and institutions from the initial point of police contact through the final moment when an execution is carried out.

Lynching, Executions, and the Moral Compromise of U.S. "Progress"

There is a fundamental paradox of capital punishment that was exposed by the Supreme Court's ruling in *McCleskey v. Kemp*. On the one hand, post-*Gregg* statutory reforms may well reflect sincere attempts to eliminate racial bigotry from influencing death penalty sentencing decisions by encasing the process "with safeguards to make it as fair as possible" (*McCleskey*, 481 U.S. at 313). However, they also empower law enforcement officials, prosecutors, judges, and jurors to make discretionary judgments that inevitably channel human error, misconduct, and an array of prejudices into the system. Justice Brennan spoke to this moral concession when pointing out that "'unceasing efforts' to eradicate racial prejudice" do not signify the elimination of the problem but rather "reflect a realization of the myriad of opportunities for racial considerations to influence criminal proceedings" (*id.* at 333). He further argued that the empirical evidence of racial disparities in Georgia capital sentencing found in the Baldus study is reinforced by "history and its continuing legacy," which has evolved away from "intentional discrimination" and toward "subtle, less consciously held racial attitudes" (*id.* at 334).

In earlier chapters, the connection was made between the modern-day death penalty and the legacy of slavery, lynching, and other state practices that have sought to institutionalize and reproduce racial caste in the United States (Kaufman-Osborne 2006). This linkage is essential to understanding why *McCleskey v. Kemp* remains such an important symbolic marker of injustice in U.S. society. According to Loïc Wacquant (2002), post–Civil War emancipation instigated a "double dilemma" for southern whites who feared that federal intervention granting new and expanded rights to the newly freed black labor force would threaten the existing racial hierarchy (and economy) by collapsing the "cardinal status distinction between whites and 'persons of colour'" (2002:46). The solution was to maintain the racial order using legally mandated Jim Crow segregation that reinforced black subservience, as well as a convict-lease apparatus that controlled black labor power through forced confinement and penal labor practices (Lichtenstein 1999; Wacquant 2000, 2002).

What we now recognize as the modern practice of mass incarceration was effectively born from the social insecurities emergent during the Reconstruction era (see Wacquant 2009), when efforts to restrict any meaningful cultural and legal progress for freedpeople became justification for increasingly punitive criminal sanctions. Extralegal punishments such as lynching extended the psychological domination of blacks through horrifying public exhibitions of physical pain that elicited considerable fear of white authority, helped maintain a compliant labor force, and denied blacks their political rights (see McFeely 1997; Wells [1893] 1999). Lynching therefore served to reassert and reinforce black inferiority by facilitating "a collective memory of terror among blacks in order to fully emphasize not only the superiority of white power but also the consequences of challenging that power" (Markovitz 2004:117–118); it also remedied the "attendant loss of the slave system's marking of the African-American body as property" by reasserting "the centrality of black male corporeality, deterring the now theoretically possible move toward citizenry and disembodied abstraction" (Wiegman 1995:94).

Lynching symbolized the maintenance of white authority during the cultural turmoil of Reconstruction and the early 20th century while the South was under federal control. During that time, black men won the right to vote, and some had even been elected to Congress, prompting violent responses from many southern whites (Ogletree 2006). It is certainly no coincidence that the rise of lynching mostly in the South occurred alongside practices such as convict-lease, enforcement of Black Codes, and *Plessy* ushering into effect the Jim Crow "separate but equal" maxim. Each signaled resistance to changes in the social order after the abolition of slavery and an overarching fear that expanding the rights of blacks was detrimental to the welfare of whites. Gradually, these practices, like slavery, faded into extinction. By the

1940s, public opposition to mob violence rendered lynching a precarious use of white authority and precipitated a shift toward more *humane* methods of racial control. Southerners began to realize that the practice of lynching was "untidy and created bad press"; the legal system more discreetly "retained the essence of mob murder" by "tacitly promising that there would be a quick trial and the death penalty" (Bright 2006:215, quoting Carter [1969] 2007).

Compared to the vicious spectacle of a lynching, which applied violent racist force to terrorize and intimidate, courtroom trials offer a more humane appearance while functioning to reaffirm white dominance. Ritualized legal proceedings legitimize the process of procuring *justice* by execution and mass incarceration as equitable and fair, in part because structural bias reproduced during investigations, inside courtrooms, and behind prison walls lacks identifiable clarity, thereby allowing injustice to flourish under the pretense of due process and equal protection under the law. The result is what Michelle Alexander describes as the evolution of a largely invisible "new racial caste system" that is free from manifest bigotry, concealed by the guise of race neutrality, underpinned by federal civil rights mandates, and fortified by a criminal justice system that is used to "label people of color 'criminals' and then engage in all the practices we supposedly left behind" by subjecting them "to legalized discrimination in employment, housing, education, public benefits, and just service, just as their parents, grandparents, and great-grandparents once were" (2010:1–3). This process of *preservation through transformation* has yielded "a stunningly comprehensive and well-disguised system of racialized social control" (M. Alexander 2010:4) and is precisely why housing discrimination against nonwhites endures despite fair-housing legislation (see Dewan 2013), proactive police tactics disproportionately target innocent blacks and Latinx (New York Civil Liberties Union 2017), black students face harsher discipline and greater likelihood of suspension or expulsion in school than whites do (Bottiani, Bradshaw, and Mendelson 2016; Lewin 2012; Smith and Harper 2015), residents of minority-populated neighborhoods pay higher insurance rates than do residents of areas with more white residents but comparable risk (Angwin et al. 2017), and black voters remain disenfranchised in many states despite the Civil Rights Act of 1964 and Voting Rights Act of 1965 (Cohen 2012; Graham 2016; Ingraham 2016; Stern 2016). It also explains why black American males such as Warren McCleskey are more likely than any other offender demographic to receive a death sentence and be executed—particularly for crimes against white victims—despite the fact that post-*Gregg* death penalty statutes outline racially neutral capital processes. Outcomes such as these reflect what Justice Powell described in *McCleskey* as discrepancies appearing to correlate with race that are inevitably part of the criminal justice system. He specifically noted that "any mode for determining guilt or punishment 'has its weaknesses and the potential for misuse'" and that despite these imperfections, the Court has consistently ruled "that constitutional guarantees are met" when adequate measures are in place to ensure that the trial and sentencing processes are as fair as possible (*McCleskey*, 481 U.S. at 313).

Jurors, Prosecutors, and Subconscious Perceptions of Racial Threat

The Supreme Court's well-intentioned commitment to eliminating purposeful discrimination through statutory safeguards designed to curtail racial bias has ultimately permitted structural bias to flourish in all areas of an ostensibly colorblind justice system. Lewis Powell clearly understood that there is "some risk of racial prejudice influencing a jury's decision in a criminal case," but he refused to mandate that *any risk* of racial prejudice is constitutionally unacceptable in a capital trial when the defendant's life is at stake (*McCleskey*, 481 U.S. at 308–309). To do so, of course, would have thrown into question the legitimacy of the entire justice system, which relies on "the inestimable privilege of trial by jury" and "the traditional discretion that prosecutors and juries necessarily must have" (*id.* at. 309, 313 n.37). Undoubtedly, the vast majority of people serving as jurors and prosecuting capital cases for the state are not consciously racist. However, stereotypical assumptions are so deeply ingrained in U.S. society that we are conditioned from birth to view people of color as inherently criminal, even if we disavow racism and other forms of discrimination (Kleinstuber 2016). This is precisely why even most open-minded people are socialized to recoil, however subtly, when passing by young, male racial minorities on the street. It is this sort of oblivious bias that becomes crystallized in racialized capital sentencing outcomes notwithstanding well-intentioned jurors and courtroom actors who complete their duties with no desire to discriminate.

The intersections of unintended bias and perceptions of racial threat in the human psyche have profound implications for the fair and equitable application of capital punishment in U.S. society. Jurists have yet to identify a statutory protection that states could implement to adequately target and expunge deeply rooted "subconscious attributions of behavior" and indelible stereotypes framing black Americans and other nonwhite defendants as inherently criminal (Brewer 2004:543; see also Carlson 2016; Collins 2002; Kleinstuber 2016; Stabile 2006; Welch 2007). Compounding matters is the fact that jurors are often unable to recognize when they and others stereotype nonwhite defendants (Ellsworth 1993; Flexon 2016). Many jurors are removed from the socio-economic and everyday life occurrences of poor and disenfranchised nonwhites, leaving them "unable (or unwilling) to understand the lived experiences," hardships, and "most poignant mitigating circumstances poor minorities have to offer, nor are they likely to feel as personally threatened by a murder of someone who is not white" (Kleinstuber 2016:40; see also Fleury-Steiner 2004; Haney 2004).

Hidden biases (and purposeful acts of misconduct) also affect prosecutors, who have virtually unlimited decision-making discretion when pursuing a death sentence. David Keys and John Galiher, for example, have found that the charging patterns and death requests in Oklahoma capital cases systematically "protect whites and harshly punish offending nonwhites" and "demonstrate that the lives of non-white victims seem to inspire increasingly limited interest on the part of prosecutors, as well as less severity meted out by juries" (2016:138). Likewise, capital case processing and death sentencing in Georgia continue to be plagued by racial indiscretions entirely similar to what was identified in the Baldus study (see Lee, Paternoster, and Rocque 2016). The task of determining when to seek the death penalty or proceed to trial with a capital case rests solely with prosecutors, who are not legally required to exhibit consistency and racial proportionality in their discretionary judgments when pursuing death (Bright 2004). Although prosecutors are barred from using peremptory challenges to remove prospective jurors on the basis of their race, pursuing the death penalty for racially motivated reasons, and making racially prejudiced arguments during trial (see Blume and Vann 2016), the Supreme Court has been hesitant to restrict prosecutorial authority "due to separation-of-powers concerns, the desire to enhance the efficiency of the criminal justice system, and the potential chilling effect on law enforcement and because the prosecutors' decisions reflect their expertise" (Vollum et al. 2015:55). Even if we begin with the erroneous assumption that acts of prosecutorial misconduct—such as withholding exculpatory evidence and making prejudicial statements to influence the jury—have no impact whatsoever on death sentencing, there are no legal mandates requiring prosecutors to show that their pursuit of death for a given defendant is proportionate to similarly situated capital cases. Yet research continues to indicate that the defendant's and victim's racial (and gender) identity significantly influence prosecutorial decisions to seek death or a lesser sentence (Paternoster 1984; Scheb, Lyons, and Wagers 2008).

Structural Racism, Wrongful Conviction, and Social Inequality

Even if it is true that most prosecutors are neither racist nor corrupt, the reality is that misconduct and ineffectiveness of counsel (along with instructional and evidentiary error) increase the likelihood of wrongful conviction in capital cases (see Blume and Vann 2016). To this point, Robert Melson was executed by the state of Alabama for three murders committed during a robbery attempt in 1994, despite the recantation of key testimony, unscientific forensic evidence that was "susceptible to bias," prosecutorial failure to disclose exculpatory evidence, and the district attorney telling the jury that "God's law required them to impose the death penalty" (Equal Justice Initiative 2017). The state of Alabama also fails to provide capital petitioners with counsel during post-conviction appeals, meaning that "Mr. Melson had to rely on a volunteer lawyer from out-of-state [who] did not properly sign a pleading and filed a notice of appeal in the wrong court, and as a result, Mr. Melson was denied all federal review of his constitutional claims" (Equal Justice Initiative 2017). Melson certainly may have been guilty, but his execution despite questions about effectiveness of counsel and the strong inference of prosecutorial transgression is troubling, though all too common.

These broader concerns about misconduct, mistakes, and wrongful convictions are not limited to the actions of prosecutors and defense counselors. In Deschutes County, Oregon, more than 1,500 criminal convictions were called into question after a crime-lab technician had stolen drugs placed into evidence and replaced them with over-the-counter medications (Selsky 2016); while in Massachusetts, a lab specialist served three years in prison for evidence tampering after mishandling drug samples in about 40,000 cases, resulting in approximately 24,000 faulty criminal convictions (Morrison and Segal 2017; Musgrave 2017a, 2017b). Similarly, a forensics crime lab in Texas was found to have applied outdated methods to analyze evidence in criminal cases (Dexheimer 2017).

Although substandard and corrupted scientific procedures fundamentally undermine the credibility and reliability of trial and sentencing procedures, oftentimes the problems go unnoticed because "the status quo is that we have scientifically illiterate prosecutors proffering scientific evidence to scientifically illiterate judges" and jurors (McCray 2017). Since 1973, there have been 161 inmates exonerated from death row in the United States, as of December 31, 2017 (see Death Penalty Information Center 2017d). Conservative estimates further suggest that 4.1 percent of inmates sentenced to death were wrongfully convicted (Gross et al. 2014). While these figures seemingly indicate that capital convictions are usually correct, they also reflect a failure to wholeheartedly rectify the corrupt, discriminatory, and arbitrary justice practices of bygone days.[3] In recent decades, several instances of questionable or wrongful execution have been identified, including Cameron Todd Willingham, who was put to death in Texas despite advancements in arson forensics validating his innocence after a house fire killed his three children and concerns that a jailhouse informant (who later recanted) had received favorable treatment in exchange for testifying that Willingham confessed to starting the fire. Further complicating the Willingham case was expert testimony provided by the forensic psychiatrist James Grigson, who claimed under oath that Willingham was a vicious sociopath. Known by the moniker "Dr. Death," Grigson provided expert testimony in more than 100 death penalty cases, even though in most of them, including Willingham's, he never met or interviewed the defendant (*Frontline* 2010).

There is also the case of Ledell Lee, who was executed in Arkansas despite the fact that he suffered from an intellectual disability (Buckner 2017). During his trial, jurors were not presented with the important biographical information about Lee's mental incapacity and life circumstances that was needed to "provide the necessary context for jurors to make a reasoned, moral decision about whether a sentence of death is warranted" (Vartkessian 2017). On top of all that, it is unclear whether Lee was denied effective counsel.

> According to an Arkansas Supreme Court hearing, his lawyer was "so impaired by alcohol" during the first post-conviction trial that he had to be drug tested. Lee's lawyer even admitted to being drunk during the post-conviction proceeding and exhibited compromised, bizarre behavior. During the trial, the lawyer was at one point unable to locate the witness room and was not familiar with his own witnesses. At one point,

the lawyer rambled incoherently, interjecting "blah, blah, blah" during his statements. His behavior became so worrisome that the State of Arkansas's counsel even admitted the lawyer was submitting the "same items of evidence over and over again." That lawyer was subsequently thrown out and new counsel was provided to Lee. (Buckner 2017)

Regardless of whether Ledell Lee was guilty of the crime for which he was executed, his case exemplifies the fundamental injustice of U.S. capital punishment—and the justice system, more generally—which the Supreme Court majority either failed to consider or simply ignored in *McCleskey*. Namely, people of color face a disproportionate risk of arrest, conviction, harsher sentencing, and execution because blackness is associated with devalued social characteristics such as hypercriminality that need to be controlled.

It is certainly no coincidence that toxic water in Flint, Michigan, flowed only to the homes of poor and minority residents; that stop-and-frisk practices are disproportionately enforced against black and Latino men, who in 2011 made up 4.7 percent of New York City's population but accounted for 41.6 percent of stop-and-frisk stops (New York Civil Liberties Union 2017); that people of color are overrepresented in U.S. prison populations and tend to receive longer sentences than do white offenders for the same crimes (Kutateladze et al. 2014; Mustard 2001; Nellis 2016; Petrella and Begley 2013); and that in states with stand-your-ground laws, being accused of killing a black person increases the likelihood of a not-guilty verdict (Wade 2013). Ashley Nellis (2016) identifies several causal factors that produce these types of racial disparities within the criminal justice system. First, discretionary decision-making related to the creation and implementation of policies and practices—from the initial point of police contact through the trial procedure and application of punishment—affect the rates at which individuals are processed into the system and how harshly they are sanctioned, for example, with regard to drug-crime enforcement targeting of racial and ethnic minorities: "Blacks are nearly four times as likely as whites to be arrested for drug offenses and 2.5 times as likely to be arrested for drug possession. This is despite the evidence that whites and blacks use drugs at roughly the same rate" (Nellis 2016:10). Second, people of color suffer from excessive social and structural disadvantage throughout life; this includes a higher prevalence of living in poverty, un- or underemployment, inadequate schooling, residing in segregated and redlined neighborhoods with higher crime rates, unstable family environments, and heightened exposure to violence. Finally, racialized cultural stereotypes about people of color and ethnic minorities inject biases into the system that encourage preferential treatment of whites and punitive sanctioning of nonwhites.

Mass media are by any measure a central component in the production and perpetuation of cultural stereotypes, in part because news and entertainment content tends to misrepresent the empirical realities of crime. Popular culture often focuses on sensational events featuring salacious details that are depicted via a steady stream of alarming examples and shocking numbers that tend to grossly overemphasis violent crime, focus on female and child victims, and frame nonwhites (particularly young African American men) as violent predators (Monahan and Maratea 2013). Politicians, civic leaders, and other public officials regularly spew sensationalized rhetoric that fortifies fear-laden cultural narratives when espousing tough-on-crime responses to "thugs" who place the lives of hardworking Americans at risk. They also play a central role in molding individual and social perceptions about criminal sanctions such as the death penalty, while also blurring the ethical limitations intended to guide the use and degree of punishment. Think about a politician who champions the need to "get tough" by executing criminals as a deterrent for future crimes or a district attorney who advertises victims' families during homicide trials, publicly pronouncing that he or she will pursue the death penalty so that offenders feels the wrath of justice. These kinds of public responses, alongside fear discourse in media reporting, help institutionalize far-reaching penal strategies as effective mechanisms for social control within the boundaries of society's collective moral compass and "may foster excessively vindictive and uncaring responses to crime and criminals" (Tonry 2004:15; see also Maratea and Monahan 2014).

Given this reality and the fact that crime news and television crime shows tend to heighten the public's fear of crime and to increase popular support for punitive penal sanctions (Callanan 2012; Kort-Butler and Sittner Hartshorn 2011; Maratea and Monahan 2016), it becomes important to consider William Brennan's argument that capital punishment is debated as much on moral grounds as on the pragmatic merits of execution (*Furman*, 408 U.S. at 296). To the extent that perceptions about capital punishment are embedded in individual notions of morality and emotion that are often reinforced by grandstanding public officials and relatively shallow news coverage (Maratea 2016; Mooney and Lee 1999; Zeisel and Gallup 1989), it is perhaps unsurprising that so many Americans continue to support the death penalty even though people of color and the poor continue to be targeted (and victimized) by a justice system that remains awash with inequality, despite every attempt to root out and eliminate discriminatory policing, legal, and correctional policies and practices. With regard to capital punishment, the most obvious solution is to abolish the death penalty because it would solve the problem of disproportionate capital sentencing and eliminate the risk of wrongful executions. However, doing so would merely displace the problem. Offenders currently sent to death row would instead be sentenced to life in prison without the possibility of parole, which is itself a death sentence that does not provide the super due process protections given to death-row inmates (Kleinstuber, Joy, and Mansley 2016). Additionally, the broader and more underlying issue of structural bias in the criminal justice system will not suddenly vanish from existence; it will simply remain concealed by the rhetorical veneer of political leaders, public officials, and other elected representatives, along with media figures and everyday citizens who preserve the status quo by championing the idea that U.S. society is based on the ideals of equality, fairness, and justice. But doing so disregards history and the unshakable ethos of white authority evident in the hyperpunitive U.S. criminal justice system that evolved in direct response to the abolition of slavery, subsequent expansion of legal rights to people of color, and the need to maintain racial caste following the successes of the civil rights movement.

Capital Punishment and the Preservation of U.S. Racial Caste

According to Loïc Wacquant, the modern U.S. justice system functions to *protect* society against outcast and marginalized groups—generally the poor and people of color—by "socially ostracizing" them via penal institutions that confine their movements, freedoms, and rights, while cleansing "the social body from the temporary blemish of those of its members who have committed crimes" (2002:50–51).

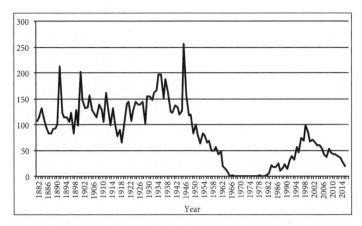

Figure C.1. Executions by year in the United States, 1882–2016. Source: Death Penalty Information Center 2017c.

Modern executions have evolved to symbolically represent the ultimate punishment that permanently safeguards citizens against out-of-control criminality and prototypical offenders. By the middle of the 20th century, however, mounting concerns about wrongful executions and the practice of capital punishment, more generally, led to a drastic reduction in the number death sentences and executions performed in the United States (see figure C.1). This gradual decline signaled what William Brennan described in *Furman* as an overall societal rejection of the death penalty. Even when the Supreme Court reaffirmed the constitutionality of capital punishment in 1976, there remained apparent reticence to put offenders to death. Only 11 executions took place nationally between 1977 and 1984.

This trend reversed course during the 1980s, spurred in part by rising crime rates, an expanding wealth gap separating the middle class from lower-class whites and people of color, and heightened fear of crime among citizens who were inundated by media coverage of drug wars, child abductions, serial homicide, and other violent crime waves that prompted skepticism of law enforcement's ability to protect their welfare. Noteworthy crystallizing events such as the violent rape of the Central Park jogger Trisha Meili and the "Subway Vigilante" Bernhard Goetz further triggered racial tensions by placing a focal lens on white victimization and perceived threats of young black, Hispanic, and Latinx "superpredators."[4] Demand for proactive policing and stronger punishments resonated across racial lines both in affluent and working-class communities. In one particularly salient moment, the real estate mogul Donald Trump publicly appealed for the five black and Hispanic juveniles convicted for the Meili rape to be executed. All five were eventually exonerated when evidence emerged that they had been railroaded by the police into providing false confessions.

Trump's declaration (and his subsequent refusal to apologize after the Central Park Five were exonerated)[5] was coded with racially neutral language, referring to "young men" and "roving bands of wild criminals" who threaten the safety of honest, hardworking Americans and "should be forced to suffer and, when they kill, they should be executed for their crimes" (M. Wilson 2002). Other politicians and public figures who supported the move toward punitive punishments and mass incarceration made similar public statements. Ed Koch, New York City's Democratic mayor at the time, reaffirmed Trump's sentiments, asserting that the teens were guilty before they even stood trial, while scoffing at the "requirement" to call the suspects "alleged perpetrators" and pleading with the public not to believe family members calling them "good boy[s]" who "never did anything" (*Central Park Five* 2012). These sorts of extreme and incendiary responses to high-profile violent crimes were hardly isolated to the Meili case. After Bernhard Goetz was arrested in 1987 for shooting four black teenagers—including one in the back—with an unlicensed handgun after the teens allegedly "approached him, one asking for $5" for their trip to an arcade, he received considerable praise that cut across racial lines. Some news reports even characterized Goetz as "a generally sympathetic" figure, even though he described himself to police as "a cold-blooded murderer," adding, "If I had more bullets, I would have shot them all again and again. My problem was I ran out of bullets" (Hornblower 1987; see also *New York Times* 1987).

The point is not that the public en masse wanted to see young people of color victimized by police misconduct or shot in the back by white vigilantes; rather, the social climate of the time gave traction to stereotypical associations of black criminality, fueled by media narratives and political rhetoric that framed black Americans as hyperviolent predators, which then became crystallized during high-profile cases with white victims. This is partly why the death penalty resurfaced during the 1980s as a necessary tool to procure justice. In retrospect, the racially neutral framing of capital punishment as a necessary sanction to combat an out-of-control crime problem masked the fact that death was being imposed according to the same racial and socioeconomic attributes that were identified in the Baldus study, were mandated by Jim Crow, and had been perpetrated in more overtly racist forms via Black Codes and lynching—the common thread being that the harshest sanctions were disproportionately applied to people of color accused of harming white victims.

Although the self-evident prejudice of lynching had long since been culturally disavowed and legislation was enacted after the civil rights movement to mandate more fair and equitable applications of law and punishment, the overarching racial, gendered, and socioeconomic patterns of criminal justice in the United States remain fundamentally unchanged, albeit with a veneer of greater humanity and equality under the law (see M. Alexander 2010; Reiman and Leighton 2010). The death penalty endures as an important symbolic marker of the modern incarceration state because it goes beyond confining outcast and marginalized criminal groups in reserved spaces of the penitentiary by taking a select few archetypal bodies and asserting total state authority (and legitimate force) to permanently cleanse society of the criminal stain that conveniently developed alongside expanding black autonomy and empowerment in white civil society.

> Along with . . . the wide diffusion of bestial metaphors in the journalistic and political field (where mentions of "superpredators," "wolf-packs," "animals" and the like are commonplace), the massive over-incarceration of blacks has supplied a powerful common-sense warrant for "using colour as a proxy for dangerousness." . . . Throughout the urban criminal justice system, the formula "Young + Black + Male" is now openly equated with "probable cause" justifying the arrest, questioning, bodily search and detention of millions of African-American males every year. In the era of racially targeted "law-and-order" policies and their sociological pendant, racially skewed mass imprisonment, the reigning public image of the criminal is not just that of "a *monstrum*—a being whose features are inherently different from ours," but that of a *black* monster, as young African-American men from the "inner city" have come to personify the explosive mix of moral degeneracy and mayhem. The conflation of blackness and crime in collective representation and government policy (the other side of this equation being the conflation of blackness and welfare) thus re-activates "race" by

giving a legitimate outlet to the expression of anti-black animus in the form of the public vituperation of criminals and prisoners. (Wacquant 2002:56)

One need look no further than the violent death of Philando Castile, who, after disclosing that he had a firearm and following police orders during a motor-vehicle stop, was shot and killed in front of his girlfriend and child by police officer Jeronimo Yanez. Following Yanez's manslaughter acquittal, the host of *The Daily Show*, Trevor Noah, reflected,

The jury had to make a decision; that decision is do you think this policeman was justified in thinking that his life was in danger? And their opinion [was] I can see why that cop was afraid. But why? Let's be honest, why would you say he was afraid? Was it because Philando Castile was being polite? Was it because he was following the officer's instructions? Was it because he was in the car with his family? Or was it because Philando Castile was black? It's one thing to have the system against you—the district attorney, the police unions, the courts—that's one thing. But when a jury of your peers, your community, sees this evidence and decides even this is self-defense that is truly depressing. Because what they're basically saying is in America it is officially reasonable to be afraid of a person just because they are black. (*Daily Show* 2017)

Noah's comments speak to the insidiousness of subtle biases that harm people of color not through acts of overt prejudice (Yanez shooting Castile because he was black) but through socialized responses (Yanez *fearing harm* because Castile was black) that devalue and criminalize blackness and are reproduced from generation to generation despite our best efforts to promote greater social equality. It would be easy to understand the deaths of Philando Castile, Alton Sterling, Michael Brown, Sandra Bland, Tamir Rice, Eric Garner, Freddie Gray, Laquan McDonald, and many others if the officers who killed them were all avowed racists—just like decades ago, when the names were Amadou Diallo, Sean Bell, Jonny Gammage, and Malice Green. It would be easy to understand why police officers who shoot and kill unarmed black men are so commonly acquitted if the jurors involved in these cases were all white suprema- cists. And it would be easy to understand why so many people of color occupy prison cells and why black American men are disproportionately sentenced to death and executed for crimes involving white victims if we still enforced Black Codes and lived in the era of Jim Crow justice. But we have made so much progress toward racial equality as a society that the ongoing reproduction of discriminatory criminal justice outcomes is more difficult to articulate when the harm occurs without any visible acts of racism. Philando Castile did not die because Officer Yanez was out to lynch a black American; he died in part because Americans are socialized to fear the perceived criminality of black men.

The Enduring Legacy of *McCleskey v. Kemp*

Within this broader social context, the ultimate punishment represents a necessary penal response to the systemic threat of black and underprivileged criminality even though death penalty advocates may not consciously support primar- ily executing the poor and people of color. When culturally framed as a mechanism of justice, closure, and the common good, capital punishment eliminates permanently a criminal menace and is posed to society as devoid of any apparent racial motivation or impetus. All of this notwithstanding, public support and overall state use of capital punishment have declined considerably in recent years amid a growing number of death-row exonerations calling into question the reliability and accuracy of the system, rising concerns about taxpayer costs for executions as compared to long-term imprisonment, and general skepticism about the crime-control efficacy of death sentences. The Pew Research Center has found that while most white Americans (57 percent), Republicans (72 percent), and men (55 percent) continue to support the death penalty (and 63 percent of respondents believe executions are morally justified), a majority also feel that there is at least some risk of an innocent person being put to death (71 percent) and that capital punishment fails to deter serious crime (61 percent) (Oliphant 2016; Pew Research Center 2015). Despite these concerns and the evident trend away from executions amid ongoing racial, gendered, and socioeconomic sentencing disparities, the practice of capital punishment remains morally and constitutionally acceptable in the United States.

Unlike mob justice, which faded into extinction when the spectacular excess of public lynching began to elicit widespread condemnation, rendering the practice noneconomical in its exertion of power over subordinate nonwhite populations (see Foucault [1977] 1995; see also Garland 2005), institutionalized forms of penal authority and social control, couched within statutory law and cloaked under the disguise of due process and equal protection, have offered a more humane appearance for disciplining people of color and the poor (see McHoul and Grace 1993). Cultural shifts toward more legal and pragmatic forms of clandestine punishments never altered the fundamental truth that racial and ethnic minorities continued to be punished more frequently and severely for criminal violations; it simply allowed these practices and outcomes to be culturally sterilized so "they are rarely recognized as racist" (A. Davis 2003:25). This is precisely why penal disparities in contemporary society cannot be readily explained by conspiratorial assertions of widespread persistent conspicuous racism, which shifts the blame back to poor and minority populations through racialized claims about differences in offending patterns that imply that black-offender crimes are consistently more numerous and egregious than white-offender crimes (see Dilulio 2005).

The suggestion that incommensurately high rates of black Americans arrested, prosecuted, convicted, imprisoned, and executed result from their habitually committing more serious crimes than whites do is a striking denial of reality because it assumes that people of color are simply more prone to criminality. In truth, the prevailing power structure functions to produce a self-affirming narrative of the criminal justice system as equitable and fair even in the face of profound evidence of systemic injustices such as wrongful executions, acts of prosecutorial misconduct, and the prevalence of excessive police force against black Americans irrespective of actual behavior (see Goff et al. 2016). In many ways, *McCleskey v. Kemp* reflected an opportunity for the Supreme Court to confront the existence of long-standing, entrenched bias born from the historical residue of slavery, Jim Crow, and the totality of discriminatory patterns and practices on which the U.S. criminal justice system was built and continues to thrive. The legacy of *McCleskey v. Kemp*, then, is not so much about capital punishment as condoning the invisible patterns of institutional discrimination and structural racism that reinforce and reproduce racial caste under the guise of colorblind neutrality and have legitimized the discriminatory application of justice manifested through crime-control efforts such as the death penalty and the ongoing penal excess of hyperincarceration in the United States.

Governments with very few exceptions aspire to preeminence and dominance, exhibiting a power to alternately legitimate or criminalize all possible processes surrounding death. Such aspirations imprint a dangerous genus of arrogance on such institutions and often disfigure the characters of people within them, whether they are offenders, victims, jurors, judges, police officers, coroners, or even executioners. While the victories of the civil rights movement helped strip off the outer layers of bigotry and rinse away the intractable messages of permanent intolerance, obligatory prejudice, and compulsory public discrimination, what remained intact is an apparatus of insidious racial chauvinism that continues to cast a pall over the pursuit of justice in the United States. *McCleskey v. Kemp* serves as reminder that the egalitarian ideal of a postracial United States is little more than a myth tacitly suppressing ostentatious symbols of everyday oppression, masking the injurious reality that implementation of every police tactic, aim of every investigative artifice, tone of every court case, and mood of every decision from the bench and jury room is bathed in both conscious and more often unconscious strains of racialized predispositions. Ultimately, *McCleskey v. Kemp* endures as an evaluative annotation meant ostensibly to save the life of one man but also in its more expansive purpose to rouse a criminal justice system and apprise its better elements to the reality that old habits of mind and racial attitudes do not fade away in short order. They are simply displaced to those social, political, and legal institutions where de jure segregation continues to flourish through the veneer of racial equality.

ACKNOWLEDGMENTS

This book would never have been possible without the support of so many people who have shaped my intellectual development and provided valued guidance. The fact that this work was undertaken at all is because of a chance conversation with David Keys. Originally David and I had planned to write the book together; but things happen, and David could no longer continue on the project. His ideas are nonetheless strewn throughout the pages that follow. I received additional assistance from several colleagues who read drafts and offered comments that addressed errors and helped improve the book, including Ross Kleinstuber, Jamie Longazel, and Giancarlo Panagia.

In recent years, I have also benefited greatly from fortunate collaboration with several amazing scholars who, unbeknownst to them, have taught me a great deal and helped shape the direction of this book: Robert Bohm, Jamie Flexon, John Galliher, George Higgins, Jacqueline Ghislaine Lee, Brian Monahan, Tony Poveda, Michael Roque, Isaac Unah, Gennaro Vito, and Franklin Zimring. Further mentorship has always been available to me in all my efforts from David Altheide, Tammy Anderson, Joel Best, and John Hepburn. I must also acknowledge the memory of the late, great Raymond Paternoster, whose scholarship is so tremendously impactful and who demonstrated what it means to be gracious and supportive of young scholars trying to make our way in academia. He single-handedly saved one of my projects despite no personal or professional benefit to himself, and I am forever grateful. Thank you all for your guidance and inspiring me to stay true to myself as a scholar.

My family has also shaped my development by encouraging me to chart my own path and embracing without caveat all of the successes and failures I have experienced in my life; and there are countless friends to whom I am indebted for tolerating what they tell me are my flaws and making my world a little less miserable, including Debra D'Agostino, Robert "*Luces Brillantes*" Durán, Dulcinea Lara, the debonair Terry Lilly, Elizabeth Mansley, Brian Owin, Jason Ordini, and Carlos Posadas. I know there are more of you than I have space to list here, but every one of my colleagues, friends, and family has in his or her own way contributed to making this book possible and helped me become a better person. Special thanks go to Dana Greene for being my most trusted fashion adviser, unofficial therapist, and a truly exceptional mentsch and to Phil Kavanaugh for his enchanting karaoke and imparting me with great wisdom on many trivial matters. I also must thank John Sullivan (and you, too, Nicole) for being my oldest and most trusted friend and because no matter how far apart we might be geographically, we always have time for the most important kind of therapy: a laugh at each other's expense. And, of course, it goes without saying of Christa Slaton, *la decana di titolo e di etá*.

Everyone at NYU Press also deserves my sincerest thanks for their tremendous support and professionalism. I am so very appreciative of Brandon Proia, senior editor at the University of North Carolina Press, for sending my original proposal to Clara Platter at NYU Press for review. No words can adequately express my gratitude to Clara for believing in this project and showing me unwavering patience and encouragement during the writing process. This book came along during the most trying time of my professional life, and its completion was delayed for longer than any reasonable editor should be expected to wait. There were many times I was waiting for Clara to tell me she was moving on to other projects; but those words never arrived, and I am forever grateful. I wish also to thank Amy Klopfenstein, Andrew Katz, and the anonymous reviewers who provided valuable feedback that made the manuscript better in so many ways. Whatever errors remain are entirely my fault.

NOTES

INTRODUCTION

1. Kirchmeier (2014) notes that McCleskey told Turner that he did not participate in the Dixie store robbery and had admitted to police during interrogation that he was present at the robbery only after officers had coerced him to confess.

2. For a more comprehensive overview of Warren McCleskey's preliminary hearing and original criminal trial, see Lazarus 1998.

3. Because this book largely focuses on the connections between capital punishment and southern history, it is important to recognize that any attendant discussions of slavery, lynching, execution, and racial injustice are not meant to characterize them as merely southern phenomena. While most prominent in the South, slavery existed in all colonies and every state; and lynching also occurred in the North, albeit in far less numbers than in the former confederacy. Moreover, in contemporary times, it is evident that racial, socioeconomic, gendered, sexual orientation, and all other forms of inequality and injustice are not restricted by geographic boundaries but rather pervade throughout American society.

4. In 65 AD, Seneca was implicated in a plot to kill Emperor Nero. Although Seneca probably played no role the conspiracy, he was sentenced to death by Nero's edict and committed suicide (Stephens 1997).

5. Cobb (1858) saw considerable irony in Nero providing slaves access to the courts, writing, "it would be a curious fact if the tyrant of the citizen was indeed the defender of the slave" (lxxxvi).

6. The victimization of Native Americans is an often forgotten aspect of slavery in the United States. For more, see Onion 2016.

7. These laws remained in force until *Loving v. Virginia* invalidated them in Georgia and 15 other states in 1967. Georgia's antimiscegenation law, passed by its colonial assembly in 1750, was among the

most exclusive of any in the country. While all antimiscegenation laws banned whites and black Americans from marrying, and a few included Natives Americans, Asians, and Filipinos, Georgia, South Carolina, Virginia, and Texas barred all nonwhites from intermarriage with whites (Spiro 2009).

CHAPTER 1. RECONSTRUCTION, JIM CROW, AND THE NEW SEGREGATION

1. The *Chicago Defender* ironically noted, "The white man is our best friend, as he has proved and as he continues to prove. And from such friends as these we still pray to be delivered. Even the years of torture and suffering can add nothing to that plea. We beg to be delivered from our friends and into the hands of our enemies, for our enemies cannot be any worse than our friends. They may even be better" (1929:A2).

2. Willie Mae McCleskey was initially charged with homicide for the shooting death of Brooks but eventually was allowed to avoid prison and plead to a lesser charge when it was determined she had been the victim of abuse and acted in self-defense.

3. Segregationists in Georgia did not quietly accept Arnall's reforms during the 1940s. Eugene Talmadge, the former three-term Georgia governor who had surprisingly lost the 1942 election to Arnall, initiated a campaign for reelection on April 16, 1946, and ran on a platform of white supremacy (Wexler 2003). Preaching to white voters that Georgia was at a historic crossroads with black empowerment, the prospect of expanded black voting rights, and a liberal federal government threatening to destroy the cultural fabric of southern life, Talmadge envisioned a dystopian future in which the black vote would inevitably lead to the repeal of "laws requiring segregation in schools, hotels, and trains—and even the laws that prohibited intermarriage" (Wexler 2003:37–38). Talmadge ultimately won the 1946 gubernatorial election but died before being inaugurated into office. A resulting "three governors controversy" ensued between incumbent Arnall, lieutenant governor–elect Melvin (M. E.) Thompson, and Talmade's son, Herman. With each refusing to concede his claim to the governorship, the case ultimately reached the state supreme court, which ruled in favor of Thompson, who was installed as governor in 1947. In response, Herman Talmadge successfully

campaigned for a special election, and in September 1948, he hand-
ily defeated Thompson and eventually served two-terms as Georgia's
governor.

4. Considerable research has been done to evaluate the efficacy of the
substitution thesis. George C. Wright (1996) determined that executions in the state of Kentucky prompted a dramatic decline in lynchings during the early 20th century. James Clarke (1998) and Franklin
Zimring (2003) similarly found that post–Civil War lynching
reflected a culture of violence against blacks that persevered through
the practice of capital punishment, which southerners often referred
to as "legal lynching" (see Clark 1998:284). Although lynching took
place in all parts of the United States, the vast majority between 1882
and 1968 occurred in the South (Tolnay and Beck 1995; Vandiver
2005; Zimring 2003). Contemporary death penalty patterns in the
United States are similarly concentrated in the former Confederacy.
Whereas 51.4 percent of all executions during the years 1930 to 1967
were carried out in southern states (Vandiver 2005:9), that figure
increased dramatically by the late 20th century. Zimring specifically notes that between 1980 and 1999, approximately 80 percent of
executions were performed in the South; this figure is eerily similar
to recorded lynchings during the post–Civil War years of 1889 to
1918, of which 88 percent occurred in southern states (2003:77, 90).
Not all research provides conclusive support for the substitution
thesis, however. Thomas Keil and Gennaro Vito contend that "support for Wright's thesis is found for the relationship between Black
executions and lynchings for the period 1910 to 1934" (2009:64); but
they also found that between the years 1866 to 1934, "increases in
Black executions did not lead to a decline in the number of Black
lynchings in Kentucky. In addition, this pattern did not hold true
for White executions and lynchings. Instead, both White and Black
lynchings were positively related to the number of White and Black
executions" (2009:64).

5. For a thorough review of botched executions, see Sarat 2014.

CHAPTER 2. MISSED OPPORTUNITIES ON THE ROAD TO THE SUPREME COURT

1. In weighing states, jurors are required to balance identified aggravating factors against the presence of statutory mitigating circum-

stances. If aggravation outweighs mitigation, they may then consider the death penalty as an available sentence. If not, they must select a lesser sentencing option. In nonweighing states, jurors are only obligated to identify at least one aggravating factor, without necessarily considering any possible mitigation prior to sentencing a defendant to death.

2. The term "super due process" is attributed to Radin (1980), but its legal origins date back to *Gregg v. Georgia* (428 U.S. 153), "where the plurality of Justices Stewart, Powell, and Stevens upheld or struck down death penalty statutes according to whether the sentencing procedures minimized the prospect of arbitrary and capricious imposition of the death penalty" (*Washington and Lee Law Review* 1982:111 n.45).

3. The National Science Foundation's Law and Science program also provided funding for additional data analysis (see Baldus et al. 1990:45).

4. Baldus et al. (1983) did find that a higher percentage of white offenders (7 percent) are sentenced to death than black defendants (4 percent) because most murders are intraracial (the victim and offender are classified according to the same racial category).

5. Anthony Amsterdam specifically described the "array of available outlets for avoiding the actual use of the death penalty" as being either "the second stage penalty proceedings in which aggravating and mitigating circumstances are either balanced of adjudicated" or "definitions of the capital crime which narrow the capital crime and set it off from others along intangible and impressionistic lines" (*Jurek*, No. 75-5394, at 11:20).

6. Although both the Cox-Snell R^2 and the McFadden R^2 were developed long before Warren McCleskey's case reached Judge Forrester's courtroom, even today there is lively debate as to the optimal method, with the Cox-Snell R^2 being preferred by adherents of the *generalized pseudo R^2* and the McFadden R^2 being preferred as a means to express proportional reduction in residual error variance. Both satisfy some or all of the requirements of an efficient R^2 as defined by Tarald Kvålseth (1985). Yet both the Cox-Snell R^2 and the McFadden R^2 were viewed as a matter of routine in the most prominent statistical programming languages of the time (e.g., SPSS, SAS) and had been the default diagnostic indicators for some time before

the district court saw Warren McCleskey's appeal. For a complete discussion of the Cox-Snell R^2 and the McFadden R^2, see Cragg and Uhler 1970; and McFadden 1974.

7. In a criticism of the Baldus study published after Warren McCleskey was executed, Georgia's statistical consultant Joseph Katz ([1991] 2012) fails to meaningfully discuss the problem of multicollinearity and does not comment on any diagnostic tool he might have used to spot it as a problem.

8. Gross et al. also find that "a major cause of the high number of black murder exonerations is the high homicide rate in the black community—a tragedy that kills many African Americans and sends many others to prison. Innocent defendants who are falsely convicted and exonerated do not contribute to this high homicide rate. They—like the families of victims who are killed—are deeply harmed by murders committed by others" (2017:2).

9. The historian Elizabeth Hinton (2016) attributes the political origins of modern mass incarceration and get-tough policing to more liberal Democratic Party policies first instituted by the Lyndon Johnson administration in direct response to civil unrest in black communities, which sometimes crystallized as race riots during the civil rights movement era (many of those riots, ironically enough, were instigated by violent policing in black neighborhoods). However, there is no scholarly consensus on this point of fact. Punitive policing of black communities and the modern hyperincarceration approach to criminal justice have been credited to a variety of social factors, public policies, and presidential initiative, including Richard Nixon's War on Drugs, Bill Clinton's 1994 omnibus crime bill that inflated prison populations, and Ronald Reagan's law-and-order crime-control agenda.

CHAPTER 3. BLACK MURDERS ARE *DIFFERENT*

1. Brennan and Marshall also referenced similarities to *Hitchcock v. Wainwright* (1985), a Florida case in which the petitioner claimed that he was denied a proper evidentiary hearing to consider mitigating evidence and that the state's death penalty was applied in a capricious, arbitrary, and racially discriminatory manner.

2. Alvin Moore was convicted of the rape and murder of 23-year-old Jo Ann Wilson. A case with a black male offender and a white female victim, the killing at the center of *Moore v. Maggio* (740 F.2d 308 (5th

Cir. 1984)) took place in a rural southern town, where several police officers on the scene said they took the victim's dying declaration directly implicating the defendant. However, it came to light after the trial that the prosecutor withheld important facts of the case from the defense. Only one police officer actually heard the victim's declaration, and Wilson's husband might have been a viable suspect but was never considered as such by the police.

3. The term "death-qualified" refers to jurors and juries who are deemed fit to consider the death penalty as a prospective sentence in a criminal case. Any jurors who are so categorically opposed to capital punishment that they refuse to contemplate execution as a sentencing option are generally disqualified from service and therefore not death-qualified.

4. While this book primarily focuses on race and social class, intersecting issues of gender are also focal points of death penalty research and merit discussion. The Baldus study identifies a statistical correlation between a victim's gender and death sentencing, although it was concluded that these disparities are "probably a reaction to the greater physical vulnerability of many female victims" rather than resulting from malicious discrimination (Baldus et al. 1983:158). Michael Songer and Isaac Unah (2006) and Glenn Pierce and Michael Radelet (2002) confirmed these findings, noting in their research that female-victim cases in South Carolina and Illinois, respectively, are more likely to produce a death sentence than are male victim cases; and white-female-victim homicides in particular have significantly higher odds of yielding a death penalty than do any other race and gender victim combination. Although research suggests that gendered effects might be related to a variety of factors pertaining to characteristics of the victim and crime severity (Royer et al. 2014), it is interesting to note that a victim's gender appears to primarily affect juror sentiments rather than prosecutorial decision-making (see Williams, Demuth, and Holcomb 2007). To this point, Elizabeth Rapaport (1991) argues that relatively few women are sent to death row, because of gender bias inherent to capital punishment law. Death-sentenced women, she asserts, are more likely to have killed intimate relations than are comparable male offenders. This suggests that the practice of seeking death in legal settings imparts "greater seriousness to economic and other predatory murder as compared to

domestic murder" (Rapaport 1991:367). Furthermore, Phillip Barron notes that women receive the death penalty "primarily for violating dominant norms of gender correctness" (2000:89); and jurors are more readily apt to believe that female murderers suffer from fragile psyches and emotional instability, which reduce culpability by making their actions seem less calculated (Williams 2010). Because prosecutors, judges, and jurors alike may simply assume that women are physically and mentally weaker than men are, they may perceive female victims as more in need of social protection and consequently sentence their assailants more severely (see Royer et al. 2014).

5. Although Powell by all accounts supported desegregation, he nonetheless at the time refrained from publicly endorsing those efforts (see Hall 2001).

6. Powell did note that death might actually be appropriate in circumstances of aggravated rape but perhaps unwittingly trivialized rape victims by claiming that they do not necessarily "sustain serious or lasting injury" (*Coker v. Georgia*, 433 U.S. 584, 601–602 (1977)).

7. Reagan did eventually nominate Bork for the Supreme Court to succeed Lewis Powell when Powell retired two months after delivering the *McCleskey* majority opinion in June 1987. Although the Senate ultimately voted 58–42 to reject Bork's nomination, his view on *McCleskey* is noteworthy. During a 1987 PBS interview by Bill Moyers, he commented that the High Court's decision in *McCleskey* was in error. Bork took issue with Justice Powell's suggestion that the Georgia legislature may be responsible for correcting any problems revealed by the Baldus study. He saw the Supreme Court majority being remiss in what he considered its solemn and primary duty "to protect the rights of Americans" (*In Search of the Constitution* 1987).

8. Justice O'Connor subsequently asked about the possibility of sentencing discrimination against females, to which Boger responded that there were "heightened" protections in place for women but that the Baldus study did not identify sex-based sentencing discrimination in Georgia (*McCleskey*, No. 84-6811, at 24:40).

CHAPTER 4. ALL DISCRIMINATION IS NOT CONSIDERED EQUAL

1. The memorandum, titled "A Random Thought on the Segregation Cases," was drafted when the Supreme Court was considering *Brown*

v. Board of Education of Topeka, which in 1954 became the landmark case overturning *Plessy v. Ferguson* (1896) and establishing de jure racial segregation as unconstitutional.

2. The Reagan administration generally favored policies that advanced states' rights, with Reagan once proclaiming in a public speech that "we have distorted the powers of our government today by giving powers that were never intended to be given in the Constitution to the federal establishment" (Stroup 2008:82–83; see also *Neshoba Democrat* 2007).

3. Ronald Reagan's tale of the welfare queen negatively stereotyped people of color and the poor but was not a complete falsehood. Linda Taylor, the woman on whom the story was based, did get convicted of welfare fraud in 1977, after she swindled the government out of $8,000. While her abuse of the system was far less than Reagan's campaign-trail exaggerations, Taylor nonetheless had a noteworthy criminal past, including allegations of kidnapping and murder (see Levin 2013).

4. Statistical regression analysis was submitted as evidence of discrimination in a number of cases, including *Johnson v. Uncle Ben's Inc.*, 628 F.2d 419 (5th Cir. 1980), *Wilkins v. University of Houston*, 654 F.2d. 388 (5th Cir. Unit A 1981), *Valentino v. United States Postal Service*, 674 F.2d 56, 69 (D.C. Cir. 1982), and *Eastland v. Tennessee Valley Authority*, 704 F.2d 613, 613 n.11 (11th Cir. 1983). In all these rulings, the trial and appellate courts seemed to arbitrarily accept or reject the use of regression analysis as truly evidentiary. At the very least, none of the decisions contained any discernable indication that the courts have consistently ruled on the value of statistical evidence, have understood the techniques of regression analysis, or were entirely clear in comprehending the meanings of the results.

5. Edward Lazarus specifically claims that "in crucial cases, narrow Court majorities transformed constitutional law on the basis of opinion the Justices knew to be wholly inadequate and unconvincing. Individual Justices sought to advance their political agendas by employing legal arguments in which they themselves did not believe or methods of interpretation they had uniformly rejected in the past. Neither side respected precedent, except when convenient; both sides tried to twist the Court's internal rules to attain narrow advantage. In short, from William Brennan to Antonin Scalia, the

Justices abandoned the power of persuasion for the power of declaring partisan victory by sweeping the chess pieces from the board" (1998:8).

6. Lazarus notes that despite efforts to limit habeas petitions, by the end of the George H. W. Bush presidency, "federal habeas judges continued to find that state officials violated the Constitution in a stunning number of capital cases—roughly 50 percent, according to some studies" (1998:504).

7. After retiring from the Supreme Court, Powell was asked whether he would change his vote in any of the cases he had ruled on as an associate justice, to which he replied, "Yes, *McCleskey v. Kemp*" (Jeffries 1994:451).

8. Justices Stevens and Blackmun deviated from Brennan and Marshall in stopping short of calling for complete abolition of capital punishment and contending that death penalty statutes designed to target only the most highly aggravated homicide cases could be applied in a race-neutral manner (Vito and Higgins 2016).

9. *Brady* violations result from prosecutorial suppression of requested exculpatory evidence that may prove a defendant's innocence, impugn the credibility of a prosecution witness, or reduce a defendant's sentence upon conviction (*Brady v. Maryland*, 373 U.S. 83 (1963)). In *McCleskey v. Zant* (1991), the Supreme Court rejected claims of a *Brady* violation, noting that "McCleskey contended that the trial court 'erred in allowing evidence of [McCleskey's] oral statement admitting the murder made to [Evans] in the next cell, because the prosecutor had deliberately withheld such statement' in violation of *Brady v. Maryland*, 373 U.S. 83 (1963). A unanimous Georgia Supreme Court acknowledged that the prosecutor did not furnish Evans' statement to the defense, but ruled that because the undisclosed evidence was not exculpatory, McCleskey suffered no material prejudice and was not denied a fair trial under *Brady*. The court noted, moreover, that the evidence McCleskey wanted to inspect was 'introduced to the jury in its entirety' through Evans' testimony, and that McCleskey's argument that 'the evidence was needed in order to prepare a proper defense or impeach other witnesses had no merit because the evidence requested was statements made by [McCleskey] himself'" (499 U.S. at 471).

10. The Eleventh Circuit Court of Appeals also determined that any potential *Massiah* violation "would have been harmless error," deeming "the State's alleged concealment of the Evans statement irrelevant because it 'was simply the catalyst that caused counsel to pursue the *Massiah* claim more vigorously,' and did not itself 'demonstrate the existence of a *Massiah* violation'" (*Zant*, 499 U.S. at 476–477).

11. For a thorough discussion on the unintended consequences of the AEDPA, including an overview of legal cases that have refined the law's application, see Reinhardt 2015.

CHAPTER 5. REAFFIRMING "SEPARATE BUT EQUAL"

1. One of the Northwestern investigations led to the exoneration of Anthony Porter in 1999, just days before his scheduled execution date, after the actual killer, Alstory Simon, confessed on videotape to the 1982 double murder. However, it was later found that the Northwestern professor David Protess and several armed private investigators framed Simon and coerced a false confession in order to secure Porter's acquittal. For a more thorough overview of the case, see the documentary *A Murder in the Park* (2014).

2. Although George Ryan's blanket commutation in 2003 effectively ended capital punishment in Illinois, the practice was not formally abolished until 2011.

3. Maryland's death penalty was abolished in 2014, with Governor Martin O'Malley noting at the time that capital punishment fails to deter crime and is inherently tainted by racial bias (Simpson 2013).

4. During a 2010 district court evidentiary hearing, evidence that Coles had confessed to the crime was barred because the defense did not afford Coles a chance to rebut the allegations.

5. It should be noted that "intellectually disabled" has replaced "mentally retarded" as the accepted terminology. Also, states established their own measures for determining intellectual disability in accordance with *Atkins*. But since these issues often come down to expert diagnosis, which can vary significantly by case and offender, there have been numerous instances of intellectually disabled defendants being sentenced to death and executed.

6. Robinson's lawyer petitioned to the state supreme court claiming that it is unlawful to reimpose the death penalty because the North Carolina Racial Justice Act hearing protected his client from capital punishment.

7. The Atlanta International Airport was named in 1980 for Mayor Hartsfield. In 2003, there was public outcry when the Atlanta City Council suggested a name change in honor of the late Maynard Jackson Jr., Atlanta's first black American mayor (Halbfinger 2003).

8. Assurances of super due process were essential to the Supreme Court's decision to reinstitute capital punishment in *Gregg* because it allows the reviewing courts during the appellate phase considerably more authority to examine whether the offender was treated appropriately and fairly during the sentencing phase. In particular, some scholars have interpreted *Gregg* to mean that states are mandated to regularly conduct proportionality reviews to ensure death sentencing is consistent among similarly situated cases (although there is no compelling evidence to suggest that these proportionality reviews are regularly performed, if at all). However, the Supreme Court has ruled that proportionality reviews are neither indispensible nor required because "*Gregg* and *Proffitt* [and *Jurek*] did not establish a constitutional requirement of proportionality review" (*Pulley v. Harris*, 465 U.S. 37, 45, 48 (1983)). Super due process has led to some offenders being exonerated or given reduced sentences. But it does nothing to address the fundamental problems endemic to the broader justice system that produce incorrect or racially disparate death sentences, such as lack of quality counsel for poor and minority defendants, overburdened public defenders and court-appointed attorneys, institutional and systemic racism, personal bias among jurors and other actors in the system, prosecutorial discretion, and so forth.

9. Citing a 2014 ACLU of Massachusetts report that black populations in Boston are stopped by city police at an alarmingly disproportionate rate, the state's supreme court ruled in 2016 that "black men who try to avoid an encounter with Boston police by fleeing may have a legitimate reason to do so—and should not be deemed suspicious" (Enwemeka 2016).

10. Jennifer Eberhardt and colleagues (2006) specifically found that white respondents are more likely to support a death sentence for defendants whose traits and physical characteristics are considered stereotypically black. In Mark Peffley and Jon Hurwitz's (2007) research, death penalty support among whites rose from 36 percent to 52 percent when met with the contention that capital punishment is racially biased.

11. These figures are accurate as of November 9, 2017, and only account for cases where one defendant was executed for killing one or more victims (see Death Penalty Information Center 2018).

12. The unintended consequences of *Batson v. Kentucky* (1986) and *Turner v. Murray* (1986) are testaments to ongoing courtroom discrimination veiled by a lack of evident purposeful motive. *Batson* bars the specific use of race as a reason for peremptory challenges to strike perspective jurors, forcing prosecutors to cloak their motives with race-neutral reasoning. *Turner* allows black defendants to inform perspective jurors that the case involved a white victim and to ask about their feelings on race. Rather than allaying racial tensions, post-*Turner* voir dire may actually encourage prospective jurors to conceal racially bigoted sentiments.

13. Established precedent barring the death penalty for crimes that do not directly lead to a victim's death does not apply to felony-murder cases in which the offender took part in a crime that resulted in capital murder and acted with reckless indifference to human life but played no direct role in the actual physical actions that caused the victim's death (*Tison v. Arizona* (1987)).

14. In concurring with Brennan on this point, Justice Potter Stewart famously wrote that the death penalty was "wantonly" and "freakishly imposed" and "cruel and unusual in the same way that being struck by lightning is cruel and unusual" (*Furman*, 408 U.S. at 309–310).

CONCLUSION

1. Duane Buck's death sentence was commuted following the Supreme Court's ruling in *Buck v. Davis* (2017). He was resentenced to life in prison for his capital murders and two concurrent 60-year sentences for the attempted murder of two others, with the possibility for parole after 40 years. He will be eligible for parole in 2035 (A. Green 2017).

2. It is not clear that overtly bigoted statements by jurors are sufficient evidence for petitioners to mount a successful constitutional challenge to their death sentence. In June 2018, the Supreme Court declined to review the death sentence imposed on Charles Rhines, whose homosexuality drew "a lot of disgust" from jurors during deliberations, some of whom "thought that he shouldn't be able to spend his life with men in prison" because "if he's gay, [it would] be sending him where he wants to go." According to reporting in the

New York Times, "some members of the jury thought life in prison without parole would be fun for Mr. Rhines. So they decided to sentence him to death" (Tabacco Mar 2018). While the Supreme Court ruling in the Rhines case might mean the Court does not view anti-LGBTQ bias as seriously as racial prejudice, the decision not even to hear the case indicates that the identifiable presence of overt prejudice directly tainting sentencing outcomes is still insufficient to guarantee relief for a petitioner.

3. For a thorough discussion of the causes of false convictions, see Ellsworth and Gross 2012.

4. The term "superpredator" is attributed to a 1995 article written by John Dilulio and focused on the crime threat posed by "radically impulsive, brutally remorseless youngsters, including ever more pre-teenage boys, who murder, assault, rape, rob, burglarize, deal deadly drugs, join gun-toting gangs and create serious communal disorders" (Bennett, Dilulio, and Walters 1996:27). Although Dilulio (1995) attributed the rise of adolescent crime to juveniles of all races, he also noted "the trouble will be greatest in black inner-city neighborhoods" and would "spill over into upscale central-city districts, inner-ring suburbs, and even the rural heartlands" populated mostly by whites. Although his theory proved baseless and has since been disavowed by Dilulio (see Becker 2001), the *superpredator myth* was advanced by numerous political figures during the 1990s and proved to be a catalyst that helped usher "in a wave of intensified policing and harsher sentences that fueled mass incarceration," largely targeted at economically disadvantaged young black males and people of color (Vitale 2018).

5. Sixteen years after the Central Park Five had their sentences vacated after Matias Reyes confessed to the Meili rape in 2002, now-president Donald Trump still has yet to apologize. As recently as 2016, Trump told CNN, "They admitted they were guilty. The police doing the original investigation say they were guilty. The fact that the case was settled with so much evidence against them is outrageous" (Burns 2016). Writing for *The New York Times*, Sarah Burns (2016), who codirected the documentary *The Central Park Five* (with Ken Burns and David McMahon), describes Trump as "apparently ignorant of our country's epidemic of wrongful convictions, which disproportionately affect minorities, and the prevalence of false confessions in those convictions."

REFERENCES

Abbott, Robert S. 1936. "Roosevelt, with Congress under His Thumb, Fails to Push Anti-Lynch Bill." *Chicago Defender*, October 10, p. 1.

Advocate. 1998. "Racial Justice Act Becomes Law: Not Soft on Crime, but Strong on Justice." 20:5–7.

Alexander, Michelle. 2010. *The New Jim Crow: Mass Incarceration in the Age of Colorblindness*. New York: New Press.

Alexander, Rees. 2014. "A Model State Racial Justice Act: Fighting Racial Bias without Killing the Death Penalty." *Civil Rights Law Journal* 24:113–157.

Almasy, Steve and Laura Ly. 2017. "Flint Water Crisis: Report Says 'Systemic Racism' Played Role." CNN, February 18. Retrieved March 24, 2017 (www.cnn.com).

Amsterdam, Anthony G. 2007. "Race and the Death Penalty before and after *McCleskey*." *Columbia Human Rights Law Review* 39:39–58.

ANES (American National Election Studies). 2016. "ANES 2012 Time Series Study." Ann Arbor, MI: Inter-university Consortium for Political and Social Research (distributor).

Angwin, Julia, Jeff Larson, Lauren Kirchner, and Surya Mattu. 2017. "Minority Neighborhoods Pay Higher Car Insurance Premiums than White Areas with the Same Risk." ProPublica, April 5. Retrieved June 3, 2017 (www.propublica.org).

Applebome, Peter. 1991. "Georgia Inmate Is Executed after 'Chaotic' Legal Move." *New York Times*, September 26, p. A18.

Arnold, Justin R. 2005. "Race and the Death Penalty after *McCleskey*: A Case Study of Kentucky's Racial Justice Act." *Washington and Lee Journal of Civil Rights and Social Justice* 12:93–107.

Associated Press. 2001. "O'Connor Questions the Death Penalty." *New York Times*, July 4. Retrieved October 24, 2016 (www.nytimes.com).

Atlanta Journal and Constitution. 1991. "I Deeply Regret a Life Was Taken." September 21, p. A12.

Bailey, Zinzi D., Nancy Krieger, Madina Agénor, Jasmine Graves, Natalia Linos, and Mary T. Bassett. 2017. "Structural Racism and Health Inequalities in the USA: Evidence and Interventions." *Lancet* 389:1453–1463.

Baldus, David C., Charles Pulaski Jr., and George Woodworth. 1983. "Comparative Review of Death Sentences: An Empirical Study of the Georgia Experience." *Journal of Criminal Law and Criminology* 74(3):661–753.

Baldus, David C., George Woodworth, and Charles A. Pulaski Jr. 1990. *Equal Justice and the Death Penalty: A Legal and Empirical Analysis.* Boston: Northeastern University Press.

Baldus, David C., George Woodworth, David Zuckerman, Neil A. Weiner, and Barbara Broffitt. 1998. "Racial Discrimination and the Death Penalty in the Post-*Furman* Era: An Empirical and Legal Overview, with Recent Findings from Philadelphia." *Cornell Law Review* 83:1638–1770.

Baptiste, Nathalie. 2017. "Imagine Being Pulled off Death Row and Then Being Put Back on It." *Mother Jones*, June 5. Retrieved June 26, 2017 (www.motherjones.com).

Barron, Phillip. 2000. "Gender Discrimination in the U.S. Death Penalty System." *Radical Philosophy Review* 3:89–96.

Becker, Elizabeth. 2001. "As Ex-Theorist on Young 'Superpredators,' Bush Aide Has Regrets." *New York Times*, February 9. Retrieved July 15, 2018 (www.nytimes.com).

Bennett, William J., John J. Dilulio, Jr., and John P. Walters. 1996. *Body Count: Moral Poverty . . . and How to Win America's War against Crime and Drugs.* New York: Simon and Schuster.

Bilionis, Louis D. 1991. "Moral Appropriateness, Capital Punishment, and the Lockett Doctrine." *Journal of Criminal Law and Criminology* 82:283–333.

Bill Moyers Journal. 2010. "Bryan Stevenson and Michelle Alexander." PBS, April 2.

Binker, Mark and Laura Leslie. 2012. "Lawmakers Override Veto of Racial Justice Act Overhaul." WRAL, July 2. Retrieved June 26, 2017 (www.wral.com).

Blake, Aaron. 2017. "Republicans' Views of Blacks' Intelligence, Work Ethic Lag behind Democrats at a Record Clip." *Washington Post*, March 31. Retrieved June 21, 2017 (www.washingtonpost.com).

Blume, John H., Theodore Eisenberg, and Martin T. Wells. 2004. "Examining Death Row's Population and Racial Composition." *Journal of Empirical Legal Studies* 1:165–207.

Blume, John H. and Lindsey S. Vann. 2016. "Forty Years of Death: The Past, Present, and Future of the Death Penalty in South Carolina (Still Arbitrary after All These Years)." *Duke Journal of Constitutional Law & Public Policy* 11:183–254.

Blythe, Anne. 2015. "NC Supreme Court Vacates Racial Justice Act Decisions." *News & Observer*, December 18. Retrieved June 26, 2017 (www.newsobserver.com).

Bobo, Lawrence D., James R. Kluegel, and Ryan A. Smith. 1997. "Laissez-Faire Racism: The Crystallization of a Kinder, Gentler, Antiblack Ideology." Pp. 15–42 in *Racial Attitudes in the 1990s: Continuity and Change*, edited by S. A. Tuch and J. K. Martin. Westport, CT: Praeger.

Bobo, Lawrence D. and Ryan A. Smith. 1998. "From Jim Crow Racism to Laissez-Faire Racism: The Transformation of Racial Attitudes." Pp. 182–220 in *Beyond Pluralism: The Conception of Groups and Group Identities in America*, edited by W. F. Katkin, N. Landsman, and A. Tyree. Urbana: University of Illinois Press.

Boger, John C. "Jack." 2016. Personal communication, July 26.

Bottiani, Jessika, Catherine P. Bradshaw, and Tamar Mendelson. 2016. "A Multilevel Examination of Racial Disparities in High School Discipline: Black and White Adolescents' Perceived Equity, School Belonging, and Adjustment Problems." *Journal of Educational Psychology* 109:532–545.

Bowers, William J., Benjamin D. Fleury-Steiner, and Michael E. Antonio. 2003. "The Capital Sentencing Decision: Guided Discretion, Reasoned Moral Judgment, or Legal Fiction." Pp. 413–467 in *America's Experiment with Capital Punishment: Reflections on the Past, Present, and Future of the Ultimate Penal Sanction*, 2nd ed., edited by J. R. Acker, R. M. Bohm, and C. S. Lanier. Durham, NC: Carolina Academic Press.

Brewer, Thomas W. 2004. "Race and Jurors' Receptivity to Mitigation in Capital Cases: The Effect of Jurors' Defendants' and Victims' Race in Combination." *Law and Human Behavior* 28:529–545.

Bright, Stephen B. 2004. "Why the United States Will Join the Rest of the World in Abandoning Capital Punishment." Pp. 152–182 in *Debating the Death Penalty: Should America Have Capital Punishment? The Experts on Both Sides Make Their Case, edited by H. A. Bedau and P. G. Cassell. New York: Oxford University Press.

———. 2006. "Discrimination, Death, and Denial: The Tolerance of Racial Discrimination in Infliction of the Death Penalty." Pp. 211–259 in From Lynch Mobs to the Killing State: Race and the Death Penalty in America, edited by C. J. Ogletree Jr. and A. Sarat. New York: NYU Press.

Buckner, Michael. 2017. "24 Years Later, Ledell Lee Maintained His Innocence in Death of Debra Reese." WZZM, April 20. Retrieved June 8, 2017 (www.wzzm13.com).

Burns, Sarah. 2016. "Why Trump Doubled Down on the Central Park Five." New York Times, October 17. Retrieved January 30, 2018 (www.nytimes.com).

Callanan, Valerie J. 2012. "Media Consumption, Perceptions of Crime Risk and Fear of Crime: Examining Race/Ethnic Differences." Sociological Perspectives 55:93–115.

Carlson, Jennifer. 2016. "Moral Panic, Moral Breach: Bernhard Goetz, George Zimmerman, and Racialized News Reporting in Contested Cases of Self-Defense." Social Problems 63:1–20.

Carson, Clayborne. 1981. In Struggle: SNCC and the Black Awakening of the 1960s. Cambridge, MA: Harvard University Press.

Carter, Dan T. [1969] 2007. Scottsboro: A Tragedy of the American South. Rev. ed. Baton Rouge: Louisiana State University Press.

Central Park Five, The. 2012. Written and directed by Ken Burns, David McMahon, and Sarah Burns. Florentine Films / WETA.

Chammah, Maurice. 2013. "Call for a New Execution Date Revives Race Debate." Texas Tribune, February 18. Retrieved January 28, 2018 (www.texastribune.org).

Chemerinsky, Erwin. 2006. "The Rehnquist Court and the Death Penalty." Georgetown Law Journal 94:1366–1383.

Chicago Defender. 1925. "Seven States Have Passed New Laws against Lynching." July 25, p. 3.

———. 1929. "He's Your Best Friend." July 6, p. A2.

———. 1931a. "Gov. Buckner Seeking Facts on Alabama." November 14, p. 2.

———. 1931b. "Scottsboro Case Stirs Europeans." July 18, p. 2.

———. 1931c. "Urges Prayer Day for Scottsboro Boys." July 18, p. 11.

———. 1932. "Lynching Record for 1932 Reaches Vast Proportions; Many Suppressed." December 24, p. 4.

———. 1933. "Reds Protest Scottsboro's 'Legal Lynching' Verdict." December 16, p. 1.

———. 1934. "Conspiracy to Kill Anti-Lynching Bill." June 2, p. 12.

———. 1937a. "Lynch 2 in FLA." July 24, p. 1.

———. 1937b. "Sentiment Favoring Lynch Bill Increases." November 20, p. 5.

———. 1938a. "Demand Action in Louisiana Lynching." October 22, p. 3.

———. 1938b. "N.A.A.C.P. Plans Big Protest Parade Feb. 11." February 5, p. 3.

———. 1940a. "Expect Lynch Bill to Pass: South Fights It." January 13, pp. 1–2.

———. 1940b. "No Lynchless Year, NAACP Report Says." May 18, p. 1.

Clarke, James W. 1998. "Without Fear or Shame: Lynching, Capital Punishment and the Subculture of Violence in the American South." *British Journal of Political Science* 28:269–289.

Cobb, Thomas R.R. 1858. *An Historical Sketch of Slavery from the Earliest Periods*. Philadelphia: T & J. W. Johnson.

Cohen, Andrew. 2011. "In the End, Supreme Court Says No to Duane Buck." *Atlantic*, November 7. Retrieved January 28, 2018 (www.theatlantic.com).

———. 2012. "How Voter ID Laws Are Being Used to Disenfranchise Minorities and the Poor." *Atlantic*, March 16. Retrieved June 3, 2017 (www.theatlantic.com).

Collins, Patricia Hill. 2002. *Black Feminist Thought*. New York: Routledge.

Cragg, John G. and Russell S. Uhler. 1970. "The Demand for Automobiles." *Canadian Journal of Economics* 3:386–406.

Culverson, Donald R. 2007. "The Welfare Queen and Willie Horton." Pp. 126–136 in *Images of Color, Images of Crime: Readings*, 2nd ed., edited by C. R. Mann and M. S. Zatz. Los Angeles: Roxbury.

Curriden, Mark. 1991. "Ready to Die, but Insisting He's Innocent; McCleskey: Skid Row to Death." *Atlanta Journal and Constitution*, September 21, p. A1.

Daily Show, The. 2017. "The Truth about the Philando Castile Verdict." Comedy Central, June 21. Retrieved June 24, 2017 (www.cc.com).

Davis, Abraham L. and Barbara Luck Graham. 1995. *The Supreme Court, Race, and Civil Rights*. Thousand Oaks, CA: Sage.

Davis, Angela Y. 2003. *Are Prisons Obsolete?* New York: Seven Stories.

Davis, Sue. 1986. "Federalism and Property Rights: An Examination of Justice Rehnquist's Legal Positivism." *Western Political Quarterly* 39:250–264.

Death Penalty Information Center. 2017a. "Death Sentences by Year: 1976–2015." Retrieved July 10, 2017 (https://deathpenaltyinfo.org).

———. 2017b. "Executions by Year." Retrieved July 10, 2017 (https://death-penaltyinfo.org).

———. 2017c. "Executions in the U.S. 1608–2002: The ESPY File." Retrieved May 15, 2017 (https://deathpenaltyinfo.org).

———. 2017d. "The Innocence List." May 11. Retrieved June 8, 2017 (https://deathpenaltyinfo.org).

———. 2018. "Race of Death Row Inmates Executed since 1976." Retrieved January 8, 2018 (https://deathpenaltyinfo.org).

Delgado, Richard and Jean Stefancic. 2012. *Critical Race Theory: An Introduction.* 2nd ed. New York: NYU Press.

Dewan, Shaila. 2013. "Discrimination in Housing against Nonwhites Persists Quietly, U.S. Study Finds." *New York Times*, June 11. Retrieved March 20, 2017 (www.nytimes.com).

Dexheimer, Eric. 2017. "Austin Crime Lab Bucked DNA Standard for Years, yet Got Passing Grades." *Austin American-Statesman*, January 12. Retrieved June 10, 2017 (www.mystatesman.com).

Dilulio, John J., Jr. 1995. "The Coming of the Super-Predators." *Weekly Standard*, November 27. Retrieved July 15, 2018 (www.weeklystandard.com).

———. 2005. "My Black Crime Problem, and Ours." Pp. 73–85 in *Race, Crime, and Justice: A Reader*, edited by S. L. Gabbidon and H. T. Greene. New York: Routledge.

Donohue, John J., III. 2014. "An Empirical Evaluation of the Connecticut Death Penalty System since 1973: Are There Unlawful Racial, Gender, and Geographic Disparities?" *Journal of Empirical Legal Studies* 11:637–696.

Dorin, Dennis D. 1984. "Far Right of the Mainstream: Racism, Rights, and Remedies from the Perspective of Justice Antonin Scalia's McCleskey Memorandum." *Mercer Law Review* 45:1035–1088.

Dray, Philip. 2002. *At the Hands of Persons Unknown: The Lynching of Black America.* New York: Random House.

DuBois, W. E. B. [1903] 1989. *The Souls of Black Folks.* New York: Penguin Books.

———. [1935] 1992. *Black Reconstruction in America: Toward a History of the Part Which Black Folk Played in the Attempt to Reconstruct Democracy in America, 1860–1880.* New York: Free Press.

Durkheim, Émile. [1893] 1997. *The Division of Labor in Society.* Translated by Lewis A. Coser. New York: Free Press.

Eberhardt, Jennifer L., Paul G. Davies, Valerie J. Purdie-Vaughns, and Sheri Lynn Johnson. 2006. "Looking Deathworthy: Perceived Stereotypicality of Black Defendants Predicts Capital-Sentencing Outcomes." *Psychological Science* 17:383–386.

Edsall, Thomas Byrne and Mary D. Edsall. 1991. *Chain Reaction: The Impact of Race, Rights, and Taxes on American Politics.* New York: Norton.

Ellsworth, Phoebe C. 1993. "Some Steps between Attitudes and Verdicts." Pp. 42–64 in *Inside the Juror: The Psychology of Juror Decision Making,* edited by R. Hastie. New York: Cambridge University Press.

Ellsworth, Phoebe C. and Sam Gross. 2012. "False Convictions." Pp. 163–180 in *The Behavioral Foundations of Public Policy,* edited by E. Shafir. Princeton, NJ: Princeton University Press.

Enwemeka, Zeninjor. 2016. "Mass. High Court Says Black Men May have Legitimate Reason to Flee Police." WBUR, September 20. Retrieved March 20, 2017 (www.wbur.org).

Equal Justice Initiative. 2015. "Lynching in America: Confronting the Legacy of Racial Terror (Report Summary)." Retrieved August 1, 2015 (www.eji.org).

———. 2017. "Alabama Executes Robert Melson." June 8. Retrieved June 8, 2017 (http://eji.org).

Failinger, Marie A. 2012. "*Yick Wo* at 125: Four Simple Lessons for the Contemporary Supreme Court." *Michigan Journal of Race and Law* 17:217–268.

Fernandez, Manny. 2011. "Texas Execution Stayed Based on Race Testimony." *New York Times,* September 16, p. A14. Retrieved January 28, 2018 (www.nytimes.com).

Finklestein, Michael O. and Bruce Levin. 2001. *Statistics for Lawyers.* New York: Springer.

Fletcher, George P. 2001. *Our Secret Constitution: How Lincoln Redefined American Democracy.* Oxford: Oxford University Press.

Fleury-Steiner, Benjamin. 2004. *Jurors' Stories of Death: How America's Death Penalty Invests in Inequality.* Ann Arbor: University of Michigan Press.

Flexon, Jamie L. 2016. "Addressing Contradictions with the Social Psychology of Capital Juries and Racial Bias." Pp. 109–121 in *Race and the Death Penalty: The Legacy of "McCleskey v. Kemp,"* edited by D. P. Keys and R. J. Maratea. Boulder, CO: Lynne Rienner.

Flitter, Emily and Chris Kahn. 2016. "Exclusive: Trump Supporters More Likely to View Blacks Negatively—Reuters/Ipsos Poll." *Reuters*, June 28. Retrieved June 21, 2017 (www.reuters.com).

Foner, Eric. 1988. *Reconstruction: America's Unfinished Revolution, 1863–1877.* New York: HarperCollins.

———. 2014. "Liberated and Unfree: Douglas R. Egerton's 'Wars of Reconstruction.'" *New York Times Book Review*, February 2, p. BR11.

Foucault, Michel. [1977] 1995. *Discipline and Punish: The Birth of the Prison.* Translated by Alan Sheridan. New York: Vintage.

Frady, Marshall. 1993. "Death in Arkansas." *New Yorker*, February 22, pp. 105–133.

Frontline. 2010. "Death by Fire." PBS, October 19.

Gallup. 2017. "Death Penalty." Retrieved June 20, 2017 (www.gallup.com).

Garland, David. 2005. "Penal Excess and Surplus Meaning: Public Torture Lynchings in Twentieth-Century America." *Law & Society Review* 39:793–833.

———. 2010. *Peculiar Institution: America's Death Penalty in the Age of Abolition.* Cambridge, MA: Harvard University Press.

Genovese, Eugene D. 1972. *Roll, Jordan, Roll: The World the Slaves Made.* New York: Vintage Books.

Goff, Phillip Atiba, Tracey Lloyd, Amanda Geller, Steven Raphael, and Jack Glaser. 2016. *The Science of Justice: Race, Arrests, and Police Use of Force.* Los Angeles: Center for Policing Equity.

Goldstone, Adam S. 2009. "The Death Penalty: How America's Highest Court Is Narrowing Its Application." *American University Criminal Law Brief* 4:23–45.

Graham, David A. 2016. "North Carolina's Deliberate Disenfranchisement of Black Voters." *Atlantic*, July 29. Retrieved June 3, 2017 (www.theatlantic.com).

Green, Alex. 2017. "Duane Buck Removed from Death Row, Sentenced to Two 60-Year Terms." KIAH, October 4. Retrieved January 8, 2018 (http://cw39.com).

Green, Tristin K. 1999. "Making Sense of the McDonnell Douglas Framework: Circumstantial Evidence and Proof of Disparate Treatment under Title VII." *California Law Review* 87:983–1015.

Greenhouse, Linda. 1990. "Rehnquist Urges Curb on Appeals of Death Penalty." *New York Times*, May 16, p. A1. Retrieved June 16, 2017 (www.nytimes.com).

———. 2002. "The Legacy of Lewis F. Powell, Jr." *New York Times*, December 4. Retrieved June 10, 2015 (www.nytimes.com).

Gross, Samuel R. 2012. "David Baldus and the Legacy of *McCleskey v. Kemp*." *Iowa Law Review* 97:1905–1924.

Gross, Samuel R., Barbara O'Brien, Chen Hu, and Edward H. Kennedy. 2014. "Rate of False Conviction of Criminal Defendants Who Are Sentenced to Death." *PNAS* 111:7230–7235.

Gross, Samuel R., Maurice Possley, and Klara Stephens. 2017. *Race and Wrongful Convictions in the United States*. Irvine, CA: National Registry of Exonerations. Retrieved April 14, 2017 (www.law.umich.edu).

Grosso, Catherine M. and Barbara O'Brien. 2012. "A Stubborn Legacy: The Overwhelming Importance of Race in Jury Selection in 17 Post-*Batson* North Carolina Capital Trials." *Iowa Law Review* 97:1531–1559.

Haines, Herbert H. 1996. *Against Capital Punishment: The Anti–Death Penalty Movement in America, 1972–1994*. New York: Oxford University Press.

Halbfinger, David M. 2003. "Atlanta Is Divided over Renaming Airport for Former Mayor." *New York Times*, August 13, p. A22.

Hall, Timothy L. 2001. *Supreme Court Justices: A Biographical Dictionary*. New York: Facts on File.

Haney, Craig. 2004. "Condemning the Other in Death Penalty Trials: Biographical Racism, Structural Mitigation, and the Empathetic Divide." *DePaul Law Review* 53:1557–1589.

Harmon, David A. 1996. *Beneath the Image of the Civil Rights Movement and Race Relations: Atlanta, Georgia, 1946–1981*. New York: Garland.

Harvard Law Review. 1981. "A Prosecutor's Duty to Disclose Promises of Favorable Treatment Made to Witnesses for the Prosecution." 94:887–902.

Hetey, Rebecca C. and Jennifer L. Eberhardt. 2014. "Racial Disparities in Incarceration Increase Acceptance of Punitive Policies." *Psychological Science* 25:1949–1954.

Hill, Jane H. 2008. *The Everyday Language of White Racism*. Malden, MA: Wiley-Blackwell.

Hinton, Elizabeth. 2016. *From the War on Poverty to the War on Crime: The Making of Mass Incarceration in America*. Cambridge, MA: Harvard University Press.

Hitchens, Christopher. 1999. *No One Left to Lie To: The Triangulations of William Jefferson Clinton*. New York: Verso Books.

Holden-Smith, Barbara. 1995. "Lynching, Federalism, and the Intersection of Race and Gender in the Progressive Era." *Yale Journal of Law and Feminism* 8:31–78.

Hornblower, Margot. 1987. "Intended to Gouge Eye of Teen, Goetz Tape Says." *Washington Post*, May 14. Retrieved June 19, 2017 (www.washingtonpost.com).

Hunt, Peter. 2018. *Ancient Greek and Roman Slavery*. Hoboken, NJ: Wiley-Blackwell.

Ingraham, Christopher. 2016. "The 'Smoking Gun' Proving North Carolina Republicans Tried to Disenfranchise Black Voters." *Washington Post*, July 29. Retrieved June 3, 2017 (www.washingtonpost.com).

In Search of the Constitution. 1987. "Strictly Speaking." PBS, June 4.

Jackson, Walter A. 1990. *Gunnar Myrdal and America's Conscience: Social Engineering & Racial Liberalism, 1938–1987*. Chapel Hill: University of North Carolina Press.

Jeffries, John C., Jr. 1994. *Justice Lewis F. Powell: A Biography*. New York: Fordham University Press.

Johnson, Jacqueline. 2007. "Mass Incarceration: A Contemporary Mechanism of Racialization in the United States." *Gonzaga Law Review* 47:301–318.

Johnson, Olatunde C. 2007. "Legislating Racial Fairness in Criminal Justice." *Columbia Human Rights Law Review* 39:233–260.

Johnson, Sherri Lynn. 2002. "Race and Capital Punishment." Pp. 121–143 in *Beyond Repair? America's Death Penalty*, edited by S. P. Garvey. Durham, NC: Duke University Press.

Kahn, Paul W. 1987. "The Court, the Community and the Judicial Balance: The Jurisprudence of Justice Powell." *Yale Law Journal* 97:1–60.

Katz, Joseph L. [1991] 2012. "*Warren McCleskey v. Ralph Kemp*: Is the Death Penalty in Georgia Racially Biased?" Pp. 331–337 in *Capital Punishment in America: A Balanced Examination*, 2nd ed., edited by E. J. Mandery. Sudbury, MA: Jones & Bartlett Learning.

Kaufman-Osborne, Timothy V. 2006. "Capital Punishment as Legal Lynching?" Pp. 21–54 in *From Lynch Mobs to the Killing State: Race and the Death Penalty in America*, edited by C. J. Ogletree Jr. and A. Sarat. New York: NYU Press.

Keil, Thomas J. and Gennaro F. Vito. 2006. "Capriciousness or Fairness? Race and Prosecutorial Decisions to Seek the Death Penalty in Kentucky." *Journal of Ethnicity in Criminal Justice* 4:27–49.

———. 2009. "Lynching and the Death Penalty in Kentucky, 1866–1934: Substitution or Supplement?" *Journal of Ethnicity in Criminal Justice* 7:53–68.

Kennedy, Randall. 1997. *Race, Crime, and the Law*. New York: Random House.

Keys, David P. and John F. Galliher. 2016. "Nothing Succeeds like Failure: Race, Decisionmaking, and Proportionality in Oklahoma." Pp. 123–142 in *Race and the Death Penalty: The Legacy of "McCleskey v. Kemp,"* edited by D. P. Keys and R. J. Maratea. Boulder, CO: Lynne Rienner.

Keys, David P. and R. J. Maratea. 2016. "*McCleskey v. Kemp* and the Reaffirmation of Separate but Equal." Pp. 7–20 in *Race and the Death Penalty: The Legacy of "McCleskey v. Kemp,"* edited by D. P. Keys and R. J. Maratea. Boulder, CO: Lynne Rienner.

Kirchmeier, Jeffrey L. 2015. *Imprisoned by the Past: Warren McCleskey and the American Death Penalty*. New York: Oxford University Press.

Klein, Herbert S. 1967. *Slavery in the Americas: A Comparative Study of Virginia and Cuba*. Chicago: University of Chicago Press.

———. 1971. "Patterns of Settlement of Afro-American Population in the New World." Pp. 99–115 in *Key Issues in the Afro-American Experience*, edited by N. I. Huggins, M. Kilson, and D. M. Fox. New York: Harcourt, Brace, and Jovanovich.

Kleinstuber, Ross. 2016. "*McCleskey* and the Lingering Problem of 'Race.'" Pp. 37–48 in *Race and the Death Penalty: The Legacy of "McCleskey v. Kemp,"* edited by D. P. Keys and R. J. Maratea. Boulder, CO: Lynne Rienner.

Kleinstuber, Ross, Sandra Joy, and Elizabeth A. Mansley. 2016. "Into the Abyss: The Unintended Consequences of Death Penalty Abolition." *University of Pennsylvania Journal of Law and Social Change* 19:185–206.

Kort-Butler, Lisa A. and Kelley J. Sittner Hartshorn. 2011. "Watching the Detectives: Crime Programming, Fear of Crime, and Attitudes about the Criminal Justice System." *Sociological Quarterly* 52:36–55.

Kotch, Seth and Robert P. Mosteller. 2010. "The Racial Justice Act and the Long Struggle with Race and the Death Penalty in North Carolina." *North Carolina Law Review* 88:2031–2131.

Krugman, Paul. 2007. "Republicans and Race." *New York Times*, November 19, p. A23. Retrieved July 2, 2017 (www.nytimes.com).

Kutateladze, Besiki L., Nancy R. Andiloro, Brian D. Johnson, and Cassia C. Spohn. 2014. "Cumulative Disadvantage: Examining Racial and Ethnic Disparity in Prosecution and Sentencing." *Criminology* 52:514–551.

Kvålseth, Tarald O. 1985. "Cautionary Note about R². " *American Statistician* 39:279–285.

Lane, Charles. 2001. "O'Connor Expresses Death Penalty Doubt." *Washington Post*, July 4. Retrieved July 10, 2017 (www.washingtonpost.com).

Lawrence, Keith, Stacey Sutton, Anne Kubisch, Gretchen Susi, and Karen Fulbright-Anderson. 2004. *Structural Racism and Community Building*. Washington DC: Aspen Institute.

Lazarus, Edward. 1998. *Closed Chambers: The First Eyewitness Account of the Epic Struggles inside the Supreme Court*. New York: Times Books.

———. 2000. "Why States Don't Confess Error in Death Penalty Cases." CNN, June 14. Retrieved January 28, 2018 (www.cnn.com).

Lee, Jacqueline Ghislaine, Ray Paternoster, and Michael Rocque. 2016. "Capital Case Processing in Georgia after *McCleskey*: More of the Same." Pp. 89–108 in *Race and the Death Penalty: The Legacy of "McCleskey v. Kemp,"* edited by D. P. Keys and R. J. Maratea. Boulder, CO: Lynne Rienner.

Levin, Josh. 2013. "The Welfare Queen." *Slate*, December 19. Retrieved March 3, 2014 (www.slate.com).

Lewin, Tamar. 2012. "Black Students Face More Discipline, Data Suggests." *New York Times*, March 6. Retrieved June 3, 2017 (www.nytimes.com).

Lewis, Anthony. 1987. "Abroad at Home: Bowing to Racism." *New York Times*, April 28, p. A31. Retrieved June 20, 2013 (www.nytimes.com).

Lichtenstein, Alex. 1999. *Twice the Work of Free Labor: The Political Economy of Convict Labor in the New South*. New York: Verso Books.

Liebman, James S., Jeffrey Fagan, Andrew Gelman, Valerie West, Garth Davies, and Alexander Kiss. 2002. *A Broken System, Part II: Why There Is So Much Error in Capital Cases, and What Can Be Done about It*. New York: Columbia Law School. Retrieved July 10, 2017 (www2.law.columbia.edu).

Liebman, James S., Jeffrey Fagan, and Valerie West. 2000. *A Broken System: Error Rates in Capital Cases, 1973–1995*. Public Law Research Paper 15. New York: Columbia Law School.

Liptak, Adam. 2005. "The Memo That Rehnquist Wrote and Had to Disown." *New York Times*, September 11. Retrieved October 20, 2016 (www.nytimes.com).

————. 2008. "New Look at Death Sentences and Race." *New York Times*, April 29. Retrieved January 20, 2018 (www.nytimes.com).

————. 2016. "Supreme Court to Hear Death Penalty Cases." *New York Times*, June 6. Retrieved January 28, 2018 (www.nytimes.com).

Litwack, Leon F. 1998. *Trouble in Mind: Black Southerners in the Age of Jim Crow*. New York: Knopf.

Logan, Raymond W. 1935. "The Second New South." *Chicago Defender*, February 23, p. 10.

Mandery, Evan J. 2013. *A Wild Justice: The Death and Resurrection of Capital Punishment in America*. New York: Norton.

Maratea, R. J. 2016. "Overcoming Moral Peril: How Empirical Research Can Affect Death Penalty Debates." Pp. 51–69 in *Race and the Death Penalty: The Legacy of "McCleskey v. Kemp,"* edited by D. P. Keys and R. J. Maratea. Boulder, CO: Lynne Rienner.

Maratea, R. J. and Brian A. Monahan. 2014. "Crime Control as Mediated Spectacle: The Institutionalization of Gonzo Rhetoric in Modern Media and Politics." *Symbolic Interaction* 36:261–274.

————. 2016. *Social Problems in Popular Culture*. Chicago: Policy Press.

Markovitz, Jonathan. 2004. *Legacies of Lynching: Racial Violence and Memory*. Minneapolis: University of Minnesota Press.

Mason, Herman "Skip," Jr. 2000. *Politics, Civil Rights, and Law in Black America, 1870–1970*. Charleston, SC: Arcadia.

McCray, Rebecca. 2017. "Jeff Sessions' Rejection of Science Leaves Local Prosecutors in the Dark." *Slate*, June 7. Retrieved June 10, 2017 (www.slate.com).

McFadden, Daniel. 1974. "Conditional Logit Analysis of Qualitative Choice Behavior." Pp. 105–142 in *Frontiers in Econometrics*, edited by P. Zarembka. New York: Academic.

McFeely, William S. 1997. "A Legacy of Slavery and Lynching: The Death Penalty as a Tool of Social Control." *Champion*, November. Retrieved May 28, 2013 (www.nacdl.org).

McHoul, Alec and Wendy Grace. 1993. *A Foucault Primer: Discourse, Power and the Subject*. New York: NYU Press.

Michigan Civil Rights Commission. 2017. *The Flint Water Crisis: Systemic Racism through the Lens of Flint: Report of the Michigan Civil Rights Commission*. Lansing: Michigan Department of Civil Rights. Retrieved March 24, 2017 (www.michigan.gov).

Monahan, Brian A. and R. J. Maratea. 2013. "Breaking News on *Nancy Grace*: Violent Crime in the Media." Pp. 209–227 in *Making Sense of*

Social Problems: New Images, New Issues, edited by J. Best and S. R. Harris. Boulder, CO: Lynne Rienner.

Mooney, Christopher Z. and Mei-Hsien Lee. 1999. "The Temporal Diffusion of Morality Policy: The Case of Death Penalty Legislation in the American States." *Policy Studies Journal* 27:766–780.

Morrison, Nina and Matthew Segal. 2017. "Prosecutors Made Massachusetts' Drug Lab Scandal Much, Much Worse." *Slate*, March 16. Retrieved June 10, 2017 (www.slate.com).

Musgrave, Shawn. 2017a. "DAs Say Dookhan Drug-Tampering Case Nearing an End." *Boston Globe*, March 25. Retrieved June 10, 2017 (www.bostonglobe.com).

———. 2017b. "Prosecutors Will Drop Thousands of Cases in Dookhan Scandal." *Boston Globe*, April 19. Retrieved June 10, 2017 (www.bostonglobe.com).

Mustard, David B. 2001. "Racial, Ethnic, and Gender Disparities in Sentencing: Evidence from the U.S. Federal Courts." *Journal of Law and Economics* 44:285–314.

Myrdal, Gunnar. 1944. *An American Dilemma: The Negro Problem and Modern Democracy*. New York: Harper and Brothers.

Nakell, Barry and Kenneth A. Hardy. 1987. *The Arbitrariness of the Death Penalty*. Philadelphia: Temple University Press.

Nellis, Ashley. 2016. *The Color of Justice: Racial and Ethnic Disparity in State Prisons*. Washington, DC: Sentencing Project. Retrieved June 12, 2017 (www.sentencingproject.org).

Neshoba Democrat. 2007. "Transcript of Ronald Reagan's 1980 Neshoba County Fair Speech." November 15. Retrieved July 5, 2017 (http://neshobademocrat.com).

New York Civil Liberties Union. 2017. "Stop-and-Frisk Data." May 23. Retrieved June 3, 2017 (www.nyclu.org).

New York Times. 1976. "'Welfare Queen' Becomes Issue in Reagan Campaign." February 15, p. 51. Retrieved July 2, 2017 (www.nytimes.com).

———. 1987. "'. . . You Have to Think in a Cold-Blooded Way.'" April 30, p. B6. Retrieved June 19, 2017 (www.nytimes.com).

———. 2001. "Justice O'Connor on Executions." July 5. Retrieved July 10, 2017 (www.nytimes.com).

———. 2003. "In Ryan's Words: 'I Must Act.'" January 11. Retrieved July 10, 2017 (www.nytimes.com).

———. 2015. "Lynching as Racial Terrorism." February 11. Retrieved August 1, 2015 (www.nytimes.com).

Niven, David. 2002. "Bolstering an Illusory Majority: The Effects of the Media's Portrayal of Death Penalty Support." *Social Science Quarterly* 83:671–689.

Ogletree, Charles J., Jr. 2006. "Making Race Matter in Death Matters." Pp. 55–95 in *From Lynch Mobs to the Killing State: Race and the Death Penalty in America*, edited by C. J. Ogletree Jr. and A. Sarat. New York: NYU Press.

Oliphant, Baxter. 2016. "Support for Death Penalty Lowest in More than Four Decades." Pew Research Center, September 29. Retrieved June 22, 2017 (www.pewresearch.org).

Onion, Rebecca. 2016. "America's Other Original Sin." *Slate*, January 18. Retrieved January 30, 2018 (www.slate.com).

Parker, Karen F., Mari A. DeWees, and Michael L. Radelet. 2003. "Race, the Death Penalty, and Wrongful Conviction." *Criminal Justice* 18:49–54.

Paternoster, Raymond. 1984. "Prosecutorial Discretion in Requesting the Death Penalty: A Case of Victim-Based Racial Discrimination." *Law & Society Review* 18:437–478.

Paternoster, Raymond, Robert Brame, Sarah Bacon, and Andrew Ditchfield. 2004. "Justice by Geography and Race: The Administration of the Death Penalty in Maryland, 1978–1999." *University of Maryland Law Journal of Race, Religion, Gender and Class* 4:1–97.

Patterson, Chaka M. 1995. "Race and the Death Penalty: The Tension between Individualized Justice and Racially Neutral Standards." *Texas Wesleyan Law Review* 45:80–95.

Peffley, Mark and Jon Hurwitz. 2007. "Persuasion and Resistant: Race and the Death Penalty in America." *American Journal of Political Science* 51:996–1012.

Petrella, Christopher and Josh Begley. 2013. "The Color of Corporate Corrections: The Overrepresentation of People of Color in the For-Profit Corrections Industry." *Radical Criminology* 2:139–147.

Pew Research Center. 2015. "Less Support for Death Penalty, Especially among Democrats." April 16. Retrieved June 22, 2017 (www.people-press.org).

———. 2016. "On Views of Race and Inequality, Blacks and Whites Are Worlds Apart." Retrieved June 21, 2017 (www.pewsocialtrends.org).

Pierce, Glenn L. and Michael L. Radelet. 2002. "Race, Region, and Death Sentencing in Illinois, 1988–1997." *Oregon Law Review* 81:39–96.

Posner, Michael H. and Peter J. Spiro. 1993. "Adding Teeth to the United States Ratification of the Covenant on Civil and Political Rights: The International Human Rights Conformity Act of 1993." *DePaul Law Review* 42:1209–1232.

Poveda, Tony G. 2016. "Revisiting *McCleskey v. Kemp*: A Failure of Sociological Imagination." Pp. 21–36 in *Race and the Death Penalty: The Legacy of "McCleskey v. Kemp,"* edited by D. P. Keys and R. J. Maratea. Boulder, CO: Lynne Rienner.

Radin, Margaret J. 1980. "Cruel Punishment and Respect for Persons: Super Due Process for Death." *Southern California Law Review* 53:1143–1185.

Rapaport, Elizabeth. 1991. "The Death Penalty and Gender Discrimination." *Law & Society Review* 25:367–384.

Rehnquist, William H. 1952. "A Random Thought on the Segregation Cases (Memo from Law Clerk William H. Rehnquist to Justice Robert H. Jackson)." Folder 5, Box 184, Robert Houghwout Jackson Papers, Manuscript Division, Library of Congress. Retrieved October 26, 2016 (www.pbs.org).

Reiman, Jeffrey and Paul Leighton. 2010. *The Rich Get Richer and the Poor Get Prison: Ideology, Class, and Criminal Justice.* 9th ed. Boston: Allyn and Bacon.

Reinhardt, Stephen R. 2015. "The Demise of Habeas Corpus and the Rise of Qualified Immunity: The Court's Ever Increasing Limitations on the Development and Enforcement of Constitutional Rights and Some Particularly Unfortunate Consequences." *Michigan Law Review* 113:1219–1254.

Rosenthal, Andrew. 2011. "Duane Buck, Race and Capital Punishment." *New York Times*, November 11. Retrieved January 28, 2018 (https://takingnote.blogs.nytimes.com).

Royer, Caisa E., Amelia C. Hritz, Valerie P. Hans, Theodore Eisenberg, and Martin T. Wells. 2014. "Victim Gender and the Death Penalty." *UMKC Law Review* 82:429–467.

Said, Edward W. 1994. *Culture and Imperialism.* New York: Vintage Books.

Sarat, Austin. 2014. *Gruesome Spectacles: Botched Executions and America's Death Penalty.* Stanford, CA: Stanford University Press.

Savage, David G. 1992. *Turning Right: The Making of the Rehnquist Supreme Court*. New York: Wiley.

Scheb, John M., II, William Lyons, and Kristin A. Wagers. 2008. "Race, Prosecutors, and Juries: The Death Penalty in Tennessee." *Justice System Journal* 29:338–347.

Selsky, Andrew. 2016. "Oregon District Attorney Reviewing Convictions in Crime-Lab Scandal." *Seattle Times*, June 20. Retrieved June 10, 2017 (www.seattletimes.com).

Severson, Kim. 2013. "North Carolina Repeals Law Allowing Racial Bias Claim in Death Penalty Challenges." *New York Times*, June 5, p. A13. Retrieved June 25, 2017 (www.nytimes.com).

Sharon, Chelsea Creo. 2011. "The 'Most Deserving' of Death: The Narrowing Requirement and the Proliferation of Aggravating Factors in Capital Sentencing Statutes." *Harvard Civil Rights–Civil Liberties Law Review* 46:223–251.

Simon, James F. 1995. *The Center Holds: The Power Struggle inside the Rehnquist Court*. New York: Simon and Schuster.

Simpson, Ian. 2013. "Maryland Becomes Latest State to Abolish Death Penalty." Reuters, May 2. Retrieved January 4, 2018 (www.reuters.com).

Smith, Edward J. and Shaun R. Harper. 2015. *Disproportionate Impact of K–12 School Suspension and Expulsion on Black Students in Southern States*. Philadelphia: University of Pennsylvania Center for the Study of Race and Equity in Education.

Songer, Michael J. and Isaac Unah. 2006. "The Effect of Race, Gender, and Location on Prosecutorial Decisions to Seek the Death Penalty in South Carolina." *South Carolina Law Review* 58:16–67.

Spiro, Jonathan Peter. 2009. *Defending the Master Race: Conservation, Eugenics, Conservation, Eugenics and the Legacy of Madison Grant*. Burlington: University of Vermont Press.

Stabile, Carol. 2006. *White Victims, Black Villains: Gender, Race, and Crime News in U.S. Culture*. New York: Routledge.

Stampp, Kenneth M. 1956. *The Peculiar Institution: Slavery in the Antebellum South*. New York: Vintage Books.

Stephens, William O. 1997. "Seneca, Lucius Annaeus (4 B.C.–A.D. 65)." Pp. 573–574 in *The Historical Encyclopedia of World Slavery*. Edited by J. P. Rodriguez. Santa Barbara, CA: ABC-CLIO.

Stern, Mark Joseph. 2016. "America Is Already in the Midst of a Voter Suppression Crisis." *Slate*, October 31. Retrieved June 3, 2017 (www.slate.com).

Stevens, John P. 2011. "Byron White—Hero and Scholar." Paper presented at the University of Colorado Law School, September 22, Boulder, CO. Retrieved March 14, 2015 (www.supremecourt.gov).

Stiegel, Saren. 2010. "How to Save Superman from a Death Sentence: Could It Be North Carolina's Racial Justice Act?" *Public Interest Law Reporter* 16:1–9.

Stroup, Robert H. 2008. "The Political, Legal, and Social Context of the *McCleskey* Habeas Litigation." *Columbia Human Rights Law Review* 39:74–96.

Sumner, William Graham. 1906. *Folkways: A Study of Mores, Manners, Customs and Morals.* Boston: Ginn.

Swift, Art. 2014. "Americans: 'Eye for an Eye' Top Reason for Death Penalty." Gallup, October 24. Retrieved July 15, 2017 (www.gallup.com).

Tabacco Mar, Ría. 2018. "A Jury May Have Sentenced a Man to Death Because He's Gay. And the Justices Don't Care." *New York Times*, June 19. Retrieved June 19, 2018 (www.nytimes.com).

Tabak, Ronald J. 1991. "Justice Brennan and the Death Penalty." *Pace Law Review* 3:473–490.

Talmadge, Herman E. 1955. *You and Segregation.* Birmingham, AL: Vulcan.

Thomas, John. 1933. "20,000 March in Chicago Scottsboro Parade." *Chicago Defender*, April 22, p. 4.

Thompson, Krissah and Scott Clement. 2016. "Poll: Majority of Americans Think Race Relations Are Getting Worse." *Washington Post*, July 16. Retrieved March 15, 2017 (www.washingtonpost.com).

Tolnay, Stewart E. and E. M. Beck. 1995. *A Festival of Violence: An Analysis of Southern Lynchings, 1882–1930.* Urbana: University of Illinois Press.

Tonry, Michael. 2004. *Thinking about Crime: Sense and Sensibility in American Penal Culture.* New York: Oxford University Press.

———. 2011. *Punishing Race: A Continuing American Dilemma.* New York: Oxford University Press.

Tuskegee University Archives Repository. 2010. "Lynching, Whites & Negroes, 1882–1968." September 9. Tuskegee University, Tuskegee, AL. Retrieved May 15, 2017 (http://archive.tuskegee.edu/).

Uelmen, Gerald F. 2009. "Death Penalty Appeals and Habeas Proceedings: The California Experience." *Marquette Law Review* 93:495–514.

Unah, Isaac. 2011. "Empirical Analysis of Race and the Process of Capital Punishment in North Carolina." *Michigan State Law Review* 2011:609–658.

Vandiver, Margaret. 2005. *Lethal Punishment: Lynchings and Legal Executions in the South*. New Brunswick, NJ: Rutgers University Press.

Vartkessian, Elizabeth. 2017. "Ledell Lee Never Had a Chance." Marshall Project, April 27. Retrieved June 8, 2017 (www.themarshallproject.org).

Vedantam, Shankar. 2017. "Researchers Examine Race Factor in Car Crashes Involving Pedestrians." NPR, February 15. Retrieved April 24, 2017 (www.npr.org).

Vitale, Alex S. 2018. "The New 'Superpredator' Myth." *New York Times*, March 23. Retrieved July 15, 2018 (www.nytimes.com).

Vito, Gennaro F. and George E. Higgins. 2016. "Capital Sentencing and Structural Racism: The Source of Bias." Pp. 71–88 in *Race and the Death Penalty: The Legacy of "McCleskey v. Kemp,"* edited by D. P. Keys and R. J. Maratea. Boulder, CO: Lynne Rienner.

Vollum, Scott and Jacqueline Buffington-Vollum. 2010. "An Examination of Social-Psychological Factors and Support for the Death Penalty: Attribution, Moral Disengagement, and the Value-Expressive Function of Attitudes." *American Journal of Criminal Justice* 35:15–36.

Vollum, Scott, Rolando V. del Carmen, Durant Frantzen, Claudia San Miguel, and Kelly Cheeseman. 2015. *The Death Penalty, Constitutional Issues, Commentaries, and Case Briefs*. 3rd ed. Waltham, MA: Anderson.

Wacquant, Loïc. 2000. "The New 'Peculiar Institution': On the Prison as Surrogate Ghetto." *Theoretical Criminology* 4:377–389.

———. 2001. "Deadly Symbiosis: When Ghetto and Prison Meet and Mesh." *Punishment & Society* 3:95–133.

———. 2002. "From Slavery to Mass Incarceration." *New Left Review* 13:41–60.

———. 2009. *Punishing the Poor: The Neoliberal Government of Social Insecurity*. Durham, NC: Duke University Press.

Wade, Lisa. 2013. "Stand Your Ground Increases Racial Bias in 'Justifiable Homicide' Trials." *Sociological Images*, December 30. Retrieved February 6, 2014 (http://thesocietypages.org).

Waldstreicher, David. 2009. *Slavery's Constitution: From Revolution to Ratification*. New York: Hill and Wang.

Washington and Lee Law Review. 1982. "Notes: Administering the Death Penalty." 39:101–124.

Welch, Kelly. 2007. "Black Criminal Stereotypes and Racial Profiling." *Journal of Contemporary Criminal Justice* 23:276–288.

Wells, Ida B. [1893] 1999. "Lynch Law." Pp. 29–43 in *The Reason Why the Colored American Is Not in the World's Columbian Exposition: The Afro-American's Contribution to the Columbian Literature*, edited by R. W. Rydell. Urbana: University of Illinois Press.

Wexler, Laura. 2003. *Fire in a Canebrake: The Last Mass Lynching in America*. New York: Scribner.

Wiegman, Robyn. 1995. *American Anatomies: Theorizing Race and Gender*. Durham, NC: Duke University Press.

Williams, Carol J. 2010. "Virginia's Execution of a Woman May Signal Shift in National Thinking." *Los Angeles Times*, September 24. Retrieved January 18, 2018 (http://articles.latimes.com).

Williams, Marian R., Stephen Demuth, and Jefferson E. Holcomb. 2007. "Understanding the Influence of Victim Gender in Death Penalty Cases: The Importance of Victim Race, Sex-Related Victimization, and Jury Decision Making." *Criminology* 45:865–891.

Wilson, Michael. 2002. "Trump Draws Criticism for Ad He Ran after Jogger Attack." *New York Times*, October 23. Retrieved January 30, 2018 (www.nytimes.com).

Wilson, Theodore B. 1965. *The Black Codes of the South*. Tuscaloosa: University of Alabama Press.

Wilson, William Julius. 1978. *The Declining Significance of Race: Blacks and Changing American Institutions*. Chicago: University of Chicago Press.

Woolfolk, Arthur. 1938. "Mississippi Mob Murders Insurance Man." *Chicago Defender*, July 30, p. 1.

Wright, George C. 1996. *Racial Violence in Kentucky, 1865–1940*. Baton Rouge, LA: Louisiana State University Press.

Wrightsman, Lawrence. 1999. *Judicial Decision Making: Is Psychology Relevant?* New York: Springer.

Zeisel, Hans and Alec Gallup. 1989. "Death Penalty Sentiment in the United States." *Journal of Quantitative Criminology* 5:285–296.

Zimring, Franklin E. 2003. *The Contradictions of American Capital Punishment*. New York: Oxford University Press.

Zimring, Franklin E. and Gordon Hawkins. 1971. "Legal Threat as an Instrument of Social Change." *Journal of Social Issues* 27:33–48.

LEGAL CASES

Atkins v. Virginia, 536 U.S. 304 (2002)

Batson v. Kentucky, 476 U.S. 79 (1986)

Bazemore v. Friday, 478 U.S. 385 (1986)

Borgdon v. Blackburn, 790 F.2d 1164 (5th Cir. 1986)

Brady v. Maryland, 373 U.S. 83 (1963)

Branch v. Texas, 408 U.S. 238 (1972)

Breedlove v. Suttles, 302 U.S. 277 (1937)

Brown v. Board of Education of Topeka, 347 U.S. 483 (1954)

Buck v. Davis, 137 S. Ct. 759 (2017)

Buck v. Stephens, 623 Fed. Appx. 668 (5th Cir. 2015)

Callins v. Collins, 510 U.S. 1141 (1994)

Coker v. Georgia, 433 U.S. 584 (1977)

Crampton v. Ohio, 402 U.S. 183 (1971)

Eastland v. Tennessee Valley Authority, 704 F.2d 613 (11th Cir. 1983).

Ford v. Wainwright, 477 U.S. 399 (1986)

Furman v. Georgia, 408 U.S. 238 (1972)

Giglio v. United States, 405 U.S. 150 (1972)

Glass v. Blackburn, 791 F.2d 1165 (5th Cir. 1986)

Godfrey v. Georgia, 446 U.S. 420 (1980)

Gregg v. Georgia, 428 U.S. 153 (1976)

Herrera v. Collins, 506 U.S. 390 (1993)

Hirabayashi v. United States, 320 U.S. 81 (1943)

Hitchcock v. Wainwright, 745 F.2d 1332 (11th Cir. 1985)

In re Davis, 557 U.S. 952 (2009)

In re Davis, CV409-130, 2010 U.S. Dist. LEXIS 87340 (Aug. 24, 2010)

Int'l Bhd. of Teamsters v. United States, 431 U.S. 324 (1977)

Jackson v. Georgia, 408 U.S. 238 (1972)

Johnson v. Uncle Ben's Inc., 628 F.2d 419 (5th Cir. 1980)

Jurek v. Texas, No. 75-5394 (oral arguments Mar. 30–31, 1976)

Jurek v. Texas, 428 U.S. 153 (1976)

Kennedy v. Louisiana, 554 U.S. 407 (2008)

Lockett v. Ohio, 438 U.S. 586 (1978)

Loving v. Virginia, 388 U.S. 1 (1967)

Massiah v. United States, 377 U.S. 201 (1964)

Maxwell v. Bishop, 398 U.S. 262 (1970)

Maynard v. Cartwright, 480 U.S. 356 (1988)

McCleskey v. Kemp, 753 F.2d 877 (1985)

McCleskey v. Kemp, No. 84-6811 (oral arguments Oct. 15, 1986)

McCleskey v. Kemp, 481 U.S. 279 (1987)

McCleskey v. Zant, 580 F. Supp. 338 (1984)

McCleskey v. Zant, No. 89-7024 (oral arguments Oct. 30, 1990)

McCleskey v. Zant, 499 U.S. 467 (1991)

McClesky v. State, 245 Ga. 108; 263 S.E.2d 146 (1980)

McDonnell Douglas Corp. v. Green, 411 U.S. 792 (1973)

McGautha v. California, 402 U.S. 183 (1971)

Moore v. Blackburn, 806 F.2d 560 (5th Cir. 1986)

Moore v. Maggio, 740 F.2d 308 (5th Cir. 1984)

Pena-Rodriguez v. Colorado, 137 S. Ct. 855 (2017)

Penry v. Lynaugh, 492 U.S. 302 (1989)

Plessy v. Ferguson, 163 U.S. 537 (1896)

Proffitt v. Florida, 428 U.S. 242 (1976)

Pulley v. Harris, 465 U.S. 37 (1984)

Rault v. Blackburn, 799 F.2d 1071 (5th Cir. 1986)

Rector v. Clark, 923 F.2d 570 (8th Cir. 1991)

Roe v. Wade, 410 U.S. 113 (1973)

Rook v. Rice, 478 U.S. 1040 (1986)

Roper v. Simmons, 543 U.S. 551 (2005)

Tison v. Arizona, 481 U.S. 137 (1987)

Turner v. Murray, 476 U.S. 28 (1986)

United States v. Cruikshank, 92 U.S. 542 (1875)

Valentino v. United States Postal Service, 674 F.2d 56 (D.C. Cir. 1982)

Village of Arlington Heights v. Metropolitan Housing Development Corp., 429 U.S. 252 (1977)

Washington v. Davis, 426 U.S. 229 (1976)

Watson v. Blackburn, 798 F.2d 872 (5th Cir. 1986)

Wilkins v. University of Houston, 654 F.2d 388 (5th Cir. Unit A 1981)

Williams v. Terry, 529 U.S. 362 (2000)

Wingo v. Blackburn, 783 F.2d 1046 (5th Cir. 1986)

Woodson v. North Carolina, 428 U.S. 280 (1976)

Yick Wo v. Hopkins, 118 U.S. 356 (1886)

FEDERAL AND STATE STATUTES

Amend Death Penalty Procedures, NC SB 416 (2012)

Anti-Drug Abuse Act of 1988, Pub. L. 100-690, 102 Stat. 4181, H.R. 5120 (1988)

Antiterrorism and Effective Death Penalty Act of 1996 (AEDPA), Pub. L. 104-132, 110 Stat. 1214 (1996)

Civil Rights Act of 1964, Pub. L. 88-352, 78 Stat. 241 (1964)

North Carolina Racial Justice Act, NC SB 461 (2009)

Prohibition against death sentence being sought or given on the basis or race—Procedures for dealing with claims (known as the Kentucky Racial Justice Act), KRS § 532.300 (1998)

Racial Justice Act of 1988, H.R. 4442, 100th Cong., 2d sess. (1988)

Racial Justice Act of 1991, S. 1249, 102d Cong., 1st sess. (1991)

Violent Crime Control and Law Enforcement Act of 1994, Pub. L. 103-322, 108 Stat. 1796, H.R. 3355 (1994)

Voting Rights Act of 1965, Pub. L. 89-110, 79 Stat. 437, H.R. 6400 (1965)

INDEX

ABOUT THE AUTHOR

R. J. Maratea is Visiting Assistant Professor of Sociology at George Washington University. His research focuses on capital punishment and the sociological implications of mass communication. He has authored and coedited several books, including *The Politics of the Internet* (2014), *Race and the Death Penalty* (with David Keys, 2016), and *Social Problems in Popular Culture* (with Brian Monahan, 2016).